KIDS,
IT'S NOT ABOUT
THE MONEY

A Parents' Guide to Teaching Their Children Good
Money Habits and Personal Finance to Reach
Financial Independence

BARBARA MONTAGUE

ONYX PUBLISHING

First published in 2025 by Onyx Publishing, an imprint of Notebook Group Limited, Arden House, Deepdale Business Park, Bakewell, Derbyshire, DE45 1GT.

www.onyxpublishing.com

ISBN: 9781913206659

A CIP catalogue record for this book is available from the British Library.

Typeset by Onyx Publishing of Notebook Group Limited.

To my amazing, kind, confident daughters, Emma and Georgia

Contents

Disclaimer   viii

Author's Note   ix

PART I: KIDS, IT'S NOT ABOUT THE MONEY

Chapter 1:   Financial Independence: An Introduction   17

Chapter 2:   The Best Conversations You Can Have
with Your Children   35

Chapter 3:   Earning   48

Chapter 4:   Saving   70

Chapter 5:   Giving   89

Chapter 6:   Spending   99

Chapter 7:   Investing   116

PART II: KIDS, IT'S *NOW* ABOUT THE MONEY

Chapter 8:   Pay Yourself First   131

Chapter 9:   Avoid Debt   141

Chapter 10:   An Introduction to Quality Assets   153

Chapter 11:   Buy Quality Assets   172

End Note   199

About the Author   205
Resources   207
Index   209

Disclaimer

The information and links contained in this book and on the website www.kidsfinance.com.au are for general information only.

The author is not a licensed financial planner, and the examples used within this book and its website are purely for illustrative purposes. It should not be taken as constituting professional advice. Readers should seek independent legal, financial, taxation, or other appropriate professional advice based on their own personal unique circumstances.

No liability is accepted for any loss caused, whether due to negligence or otherwise, arising from the use of the information, including any statement, opinion, error, or omission provided directly or indirectly, by the use of the website or the book.

Please refer to the product Disclosure Statement before investing in any of the products mentioned.

This information is current as at the date of publication.

Author's Note

As parents, we want to give our children the best possible start in life so that by the time they hit adulthood, they are prepared for the future and have a multitude of options available to them. We want them to live life on their own terms; to be who they want to be; to enjoy their chosen profession.

This often requires financial independence—and financial independence requires earning, saving, investing in quality assets, and avoiding unnecessary debt.

Why should we aspire for our children to be financially independent by the time they hit adulthood? Well, let's take my case as an example: I finished working when I was pregnant with my first child, and I haven't returned to full-time work since, as the income I receive from my investment properties and the dividends from my portfolios is higher than my living expenses. My husband also took two years off work while our girls were young, and we could afford to do this because we had an adequate 'buffer' cash account. (We'll talk about this in more detail a little later!) This was a very fortunate position for us to be in, and is one of the reasons why I have chosen to write this book: I want to teach our children (and help other parents to teach *their* children) the fundamental lessons of personal finance and the actions required to achieve financial independence.

Sometimes parents don't know where to start with personal finance: the finance world can be confusing, and so is its terminology. But *it doesn't need to be*. I believe that personal finance can (and *should*) be taught to children as young as five, and you can start doing this by using the strategies outlined in this book.

While it is notable that I am not a qualified financial planner (I am a mum and an engineer with an affinity for personal finance!), the purpose of this book is to provide you with a roadmap/clear plan of the basic skills and knowledge you need in order to teach your kids about the financial world in such a way where you can ensure that they are set up as well as possible when they hit adulthood. After all, there is no better teacher of life lessons for your children than yourself!

Armed with valuable knowledge and the correct tools, you can equip your child to spend and invest wisely in their adulthood... which also means more time to focus on enjoying life *without* worrying about finances.

First, though, you need to be kind to yourself. You will make mistakes and learn along with your child. My suggestions and examples used throughout this book are a guide only, and you should adjust them to suit your own situation. Take small steps or take a break if needed, but keep moving forward.

Part I of this book is about using money to instil values and build the foundational steps which underpin financial independence while your children are still young so they can achieve financial success later in life.

Part II is aimed at teenagers who already have these foundational steps in place and are working their first part-time job, and are thus looking for the most direct path to financial independence.

In these sections, I will explain how and when I introduced pocket money and how to use money as a tool to teach values such as patience, kindness, and determination, and, of course, we will also discuss investing and what working towards reaching tangible financial independence looks like.

Stage 1: Kids, It's Not About the Money
(Parents Teaching Values Through Pocket Money)

Children Aged 0-14

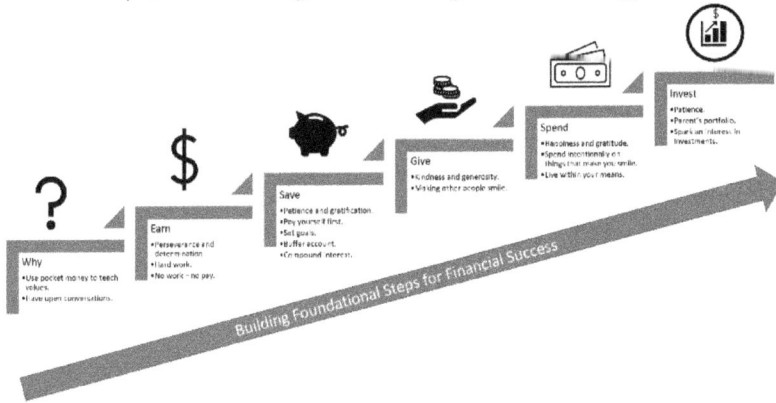

Building Foundational Steps for Financial Success

Why
- Use pocket money to teach values.
- Have open conversations.

Earn
- Perseverance and determination.
- Hard work.
- No work - no pay.

Save
- Patience and gratification.
- Pay yourself first.
- Set goals.
- Buffer account.
- Compound interest.

Give
- Kindness and generosity.
- Making other people smile.

Spend
- Happiness and gratitude.
- Spend intentionally on things that make you smile.
- Live within your means.

Invest
- Patience.
- Parent's portfolio.
- Spark an interest in investments.

Stage 2: Kids, It's *Now* About the Money
(Framework for Financial Independence)

Older Children Aged 14+

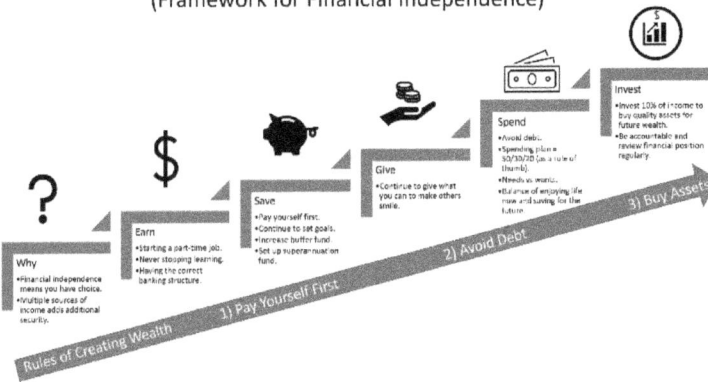

Rules of Creating Wealth

1) Pay Yourself First

2) Avoid Debt

3) Buy Assets

Why
- Financial independence means you have choice.
- Multiple sources of income adds additional security.

Earn
- Starting a part-time job.
- Never stopping learning.
- Having the correct banking structure.

Save
- Pay yourself first.
- Continue to set goals.
- Increase buffer fund.
- Set up superannuation fund.

Give
- Continue to give what you can to make others smile.

Spend
- Avoid debt.
- Spending plan = 50/30/20 (as a rule of thumb).
- Needs vs wants.
- Balance of enjoying life now and saving for the future.

Invest
- Invest 10% of income to buy quality assets for future wealth.
- Be accountable and review financial position regularly.

By reading this book, you're taking the first crucial step in developing your family's roadmap... but this doesn't mean reading is enough on its own. To get the results you desire, you need knowledge and action. To help keep you on track with this, I have given you a list of activities to complete at the end of each major section.

Imagine your child having the choice of where to work and how often and having the confidence to make financial decisions so they can live the life they dream of. Talk about every parent's wish—and that's *completely* achievable, right here, right now.

Let's get into it.

PART I

KIDS, IT'S NOT ABOUT THE MONEY

1

Financial Independence: An Introduction

As parents, we want what's best for our kids, and one of the greatest gifts we can give them is the gift of choice—the ability to choose what they want to study, which source of income to pursue, or where they want to live. Financial independence = having the means to decide how you spend your time, into adulthood and beyond.

Have you ever looked in the mirror and thought, *I wish I didn't have to go to work today so I could spend more time with my kids*? If you have, you're not alone: after parental leave (as in, maternity and paternity leave) finishes, most parents only return to full time work because they need the money.

In other words, they return to work because they don't have any other choice.

Now, imagine if you could have taken an extended break from your career for those first few years of your child's life—or, if you wanted to, continued to work, but only during hours that suited your family and because you *wanted* to work, not because you *had* to.

Well, financially independent people *have this choice*.

To set the stage for everything else we're going to explore in this book, this chapter will explain what financial independence is and why it is essential to teach your children about personal finance (even if you don't think you know a lot about it yourself). After all, to become financially independent, you need time, an understanding of personal finance, and a willingness to take action. When we have these things, we can optimise our children's chances of living a life of choice by being open to this and taking the time to teach them vital financial skills.

Let's begin our teachings by looking at an anecdote.

A good friend of mine, Erin, is a terrific mum, and she wants to give her daughter, Isla, the best life that she possibly can. It's evident that they have a close connection and mutual respect.

Erin wishes that she could spend more time with Isla and enrol her in dance lessons and gymnastics, but unfortunately, she needs to work five days a week to cover their living expenses, and she lives from one pay check to the next, meaning there is no spare cash for extra lessons, and *definitely* no flexibility to put money aside for saving. Erin isn't poor: she has a lovely house, lives a good life, and is a very clever and dedicated mum. Her money just doesn't stretch more than a week or two in advance.

Essentially, Erin is worried that her daughter will inherit her (lack of) money management skills and knowledge in personal finance—and Erin worries that neither she nor her daughter will escape the negative cycle of working, spending, and paying off debt as a result.

It is important to note that Erin never heard her parents talk about money when she was growing up. It didn't cause any household stress, but was simply never discussed at home or at any time through her schooling. Hence, Erin just assumed it was something she didn't need to know about. Her parents simply told her to finish school, get a job, and take it from there. Foolproof, right?

Erin wasn't naïve about investments, however: she knew that her friends had invested in shares and had some investment properties, and one friend even almost convinced her to invest in cryptocurrency. Yet the problem was that *it was all too confusing*. There were too many options, and she didn't know how to start or if she would ever have enough money to bother with it.

What Erin needed was to understand the basics of personal finance and gain financial independence.

But what does 'financial independence' mean, exactly?

There are a lot of different definitions of financial security, independence, and freedom. I personally define financial independence as 'having enough passive income to cover your current lifestyle without being employed or dependent on others for the period you plan'. It is a tangible goal. Financial *freedom*, on the other hand, is a mindset. It can be defined as 'having enough passive income to cover the life you *dream* about'— though it can also mean different things to different people.

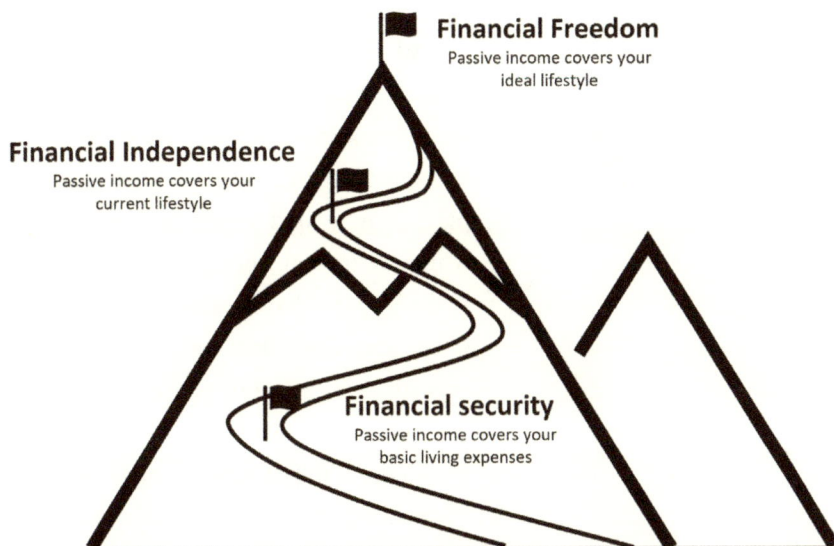

Financial Freedom
Passive income covers your
ideal lifestyle

Financial Independence
Passive income covers your
current lifestyle

Financial security
Passive income covers your
basic living expenses

From a parent's perspective, we want our children to live the lifestyle they dream about—in which case, financial independence and financial freedom are interchangeable. This book will refer to this as 'financial independence'. It will give you and your children innumerable options in life—but before we get into the 'how' tactics, it is first beneficial to first consider the 'why'.

As a generalisation, we were always told to:

1. Attend school.
2. Get a good job.
3. Get married, buy a house, and have kids (though not necessarily in that order).
4. Continue working to pay *off* that house and put some money into superannuation.
5. Retire in your sixties and hope that you have enough money saved to last until you pass away.

This financial life ends up looking a little something like this:

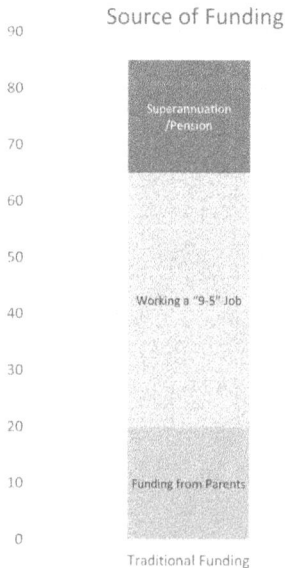

Source of Funding

90
80
Superannuation /Pension
70
60
50
Working a "9-5" Job
40
30
20
10
Funding from Parents
0

Traditional Funding

Now, there is no problem with the above path—but what if there was an alternative? A path that we might not have known existed when we were younger? A path that could present the possibility of us having mini retirements (i.e., an intentionally planned extended period away from work) while we're still young enough to enjoy them? A path that means we don't have to stress about whether we're going to have enough money in our retirement fund by the time we leave work because the government might have changed the 'rules' by that point?

And no, I'm not referring to winning

the lotto or receiving a lump sum of inheritance or a huge payout. Instead, I'm referring to *changing your funding source,* as shown in the following diagram.

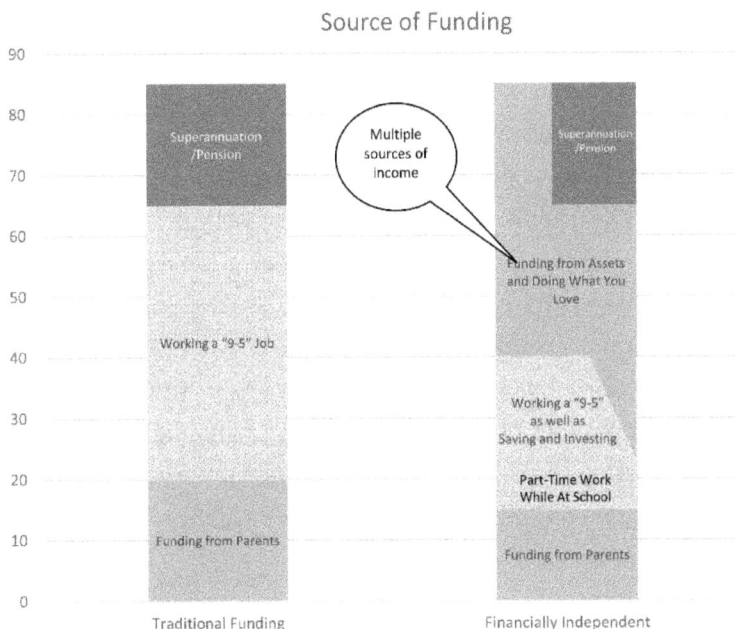

Source of Funding

90			
80	Superannuation /Pension	Multiple sources of income	Superannuation /Pension
70			
60			
50			Funding from Assets and Doing What You Love
40	Working a "9-5" Job		
30			Working a "9-5" as well as Saving and Investing
20			Part-Time Work While At School
10	Funding from Parents		Funding from Parents
0			
	Traditional Funding		Financially Independent

If our funding comes from multiple sources, including our assets, this means that we *do* have choices: we can choose to continue to work in our current job; we can choose to change careers; we can choose to go on a holiday; we can choose to sleep in every day.

Therefore, the reason why becoming financially independent is so important is because it means we can *gain the freedom to live the lifestyle that we want.*

'But where are these magical money-creating assets?' I hear you asking. Unfortunately, they don't appear by magic: you need to work hard, give what you can, and then save and invest in quality assets... all while avoiding bad debt.

Sounds like a lot of steps, right? Don't worry, we will take it slowly, step by tiny step. The first thing to understand is what the three vital elements to achieving final independence are. We will go through each in detail later in the book, but to provide you with an executive summary to get you started, these are:

1. Understanding personal finance. This book will provide you with the essential elements of personal finance that you *need* to learn, and then you will be able to teach these to your children.

2. Time. Don't look back at the past. Instead, you should begin your journey by planning from today. It's never too late to change your financial pathway and become financially independent. This doesn't mean, however, that the lessons we learned as a child won't form habits that can eventually become a lifestyle—hence why educating our younger generations about this subject is so important! The sooner you start, the greater the opportunities.

3. Taking action. You need to give your children the courage and knowledge to act.

It is also important to remember that financial independence looks different for everyone. For example:

- Financial independence for a couple in their sixties might mean living debt-free and having a combination of enough superannuation and an extensive share portfolio where they can gradually sell off and enjoy a luxury lifestyle (i.e., annual holidays, an upgraded car every five years or so, and frequent dining out), without them ever needing to go to work.

- For me, financial independence meant maintaining our current lifestyle while taking five to ten years away from my career to be with my children full-time. This also meant having the freedom to be able to work part-time in a job that I love because I *want* to work, not because I *have* to. It also meant only working during school hours, so I could be available for my children.

- Financial independence for a twenty-year-old might mean working remotely on their online business while travelling around Australia for twelve months.

- For a five-year-old, financial independence might be reaching their savings goal to buy a toy that they've been wanting, all while still being able to buy a lollipop after swimming lessons each week.

In each of these cases, financial independence essentially means that you can have the lifestyle you want for the period you have planned for, without being forced to do something you don't want to do.

There are many different pathways to financial independence, and, as previously mentioned, the purpose of this book is to provide you with a roadmap so you can teach your children how to take the most direct route to financial independence—and you will develop this financial independence roadmap in stages.

The most significant step for parents is setting up and maintaining Stage 1, the Foundation Roadmap. Many parents teach their children values and instil solid financial habits using pocket money, and this book will help to guide you through each part of the Foundation Roadmap via practical examples and meaningful conversations you can have with your children.

Now, before we dive into the details of how to set up and implement the Foundation Roadmap, let's briefly remind ourselves of the three elements required to become financially independent:

1. Understanding personal finance (which is simply learning how to manage our money and get the most out of it).

2. Time (and the sooner you and your children start, the better!).

3. Taking action (and the sooner you choose to act, the sooner you'll become financially stable and be able to teach your children to do the same).

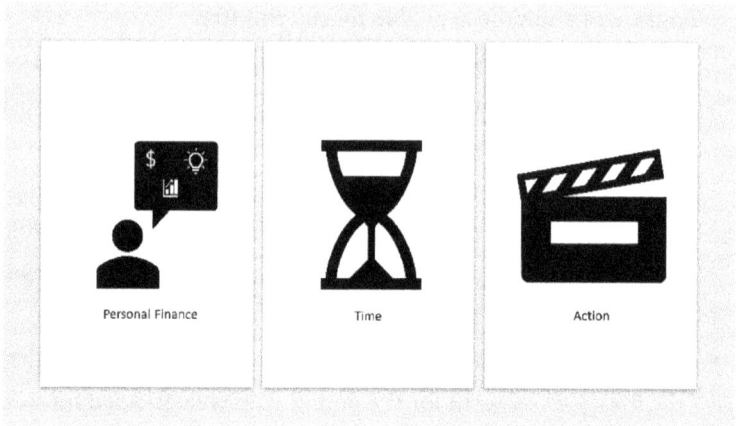

| Personal Finance | Time | Action |

Let's tackle each of these below.

Personal Finance

Some financial terminology can seem overwhelming and confusing at first sight, and this often leads parents down a path where they don't know where to start or have the confidence to make big financial decisions for their kids.

Case in point: have you ever been in a conversation where someone said, 'I want to start saving for my kids' education, but where do I put my money? Bank accounts, managed funds, or somewhere else?' If so, this proves that these decisions often just feel too hard: there are so many options that you just feel paralysed, or you don't think you have enough money to follow through with the option you feel is best, so you end up doing... nothing. Then, several years later, the same questions are still being asked, and no headway has been made!

If this sounds a little like you, what I want you to remember is that personal finance is precisely what it says: personal. So don't compare your situation to others': everyone has a different capacity to earn, save, give, and invest!

To stack the cards against us further, many of us live in a culture where money is considered a taboo topic, and in these environments, nobody discusses how much they earn or what they paid for their kid's latest toy— which is very frustrating, as a lot of our problems and confusion surrounding personal finance would be solved if we were humble but honest about our money, especially with our children and immediate family. Contrary to popular belief, you won't raise spoilt children by merely talking about money with them!

This doesn't mean we need to obsess over money or talk about it all the time; instead, we need to intentionally create 'teachable moments' which will instil the values we want our children to have—most notably, kindness.

So, to help break down the finance world for you a little bit and give you a solid place to start, this book will explore each aspect of personal finance that you need to be aware of in order to understand and develop your child's Foundation Roadmap.

Remember, everyone's situation is different, so you can take my teachings and rework them in a way that is more compatible with you and your family. I'll give you examples from my personal experience to put your learning into context, but when it's time for you to make decisions, the best gauge to use is the question, 'Will this decision still allow me to sleep at night?'

For example, the amount you have in your 'buffer account' (we'll discuss this later!) might be one thousand dollars, or it might be ten thousand dollars, and while I will give you the rough guidelines that I have used, it's important to keep in mind that I am not a financial planner, so it is illegal for me to provide you with specific advice without direct knowledge of your circumstances.

Bottom line: personal finance doesn't need to be complicated. Personal finance can (and I believe *should*) be taught to children as young as five years old. Unfortunately, however, this is not something that is covered in depth at school, and so as parents, it's up to us (and us alone!) to teach our children these critical life skills.

Remember:

> *Financial success is knowing how to get the most out of your money. The concept remains the same for a five-year-old and a fifty-year-old.*

Time

Regardless of your current financial situation or what's going on in the world—from the COVID-19 pandemic to Global Financial Crisis (GFC)—the one thing that your children have in their favour is time! The more time you have (assuming educated decisions and risk management strategies are put in place—but more on this later), the more significant your ability to generate wealth will be.

Time is critical on three fronts:

1. The repeated lessons you learn early become intrinsic habits. Therefore, teaching our children good financial habits (e.g., saving and budgeting) is one of the best ways in which you can prepare them for a secure and stable financial future. But remember, a behaviour will only become a habit if it is repeated enough times to become automatic. Accordingly, these lessons are not designed to be taught only once; you need to continually find opportunities to teach and learn from mistakes. Notably, children learn through watching more than listening, so it is vital that you walk the talk.

2. Investing over a longer timeframe, such as over ten years, will allow you to 'ride out' the stock market or property cycle through the highs and lows and increase the value of your stock portfolio over time, all while selling your stocks when a profit has been made on your shares and at a time that suits you. This is why

superannuation/401K funds generally have a high percentage of funds invested in the stock market for younger generations who have a longer timeframe to invest, while they encourage people close to retirement age to have a higher rate in cash and bonds in case the stock market goes down and doesn't have time to recover when the retirees need their money.

(Note: Stock markets and property prices are not guaranteed to increase. However, historically, this has remained the case, and so one can pretty confidently assume the cycle will continue to repeat itself.)

3. Time is what gives compound interest its magic. According to Einstein, 'Compound interest is the eighth wonder of the world. He who understands it earns it [...] he who doesn't [...] pays it.' Compound interest works slightly differently to simple interest: instead of simply earning interest on the principal amount (initial deposit), it allows one to earn money on the interest accrued each month. By doing this, it has the capacity to *really* boost savings. Conversely, if you owe money and the interest is compounding, the debt can start to add up quickly.

To expand on (3), consider the following example: an initial deposit (the principal amount) of one thousand dollars is invested at eight percent interest per annum. Simple interest would be eight percent of one thousand dollars—so eighty dollars per year. This means that the balance would be one thousand eight hundred dollars after ten years, two thousand six hundred dollars after twenty years, five thousand dollars after fifty years, and so on. However, with compound interest, the balance doubles in value approximately every ten years, with *no* further deposits. This means after ten years, the balance would be approximately two thousand dollars; after twenty years, four thousand five hundred dollars; after thirty years, ten thousand dollars; after forty years, twenty-two thousand dollars; and after fifty years, forty-six thousand dollars.

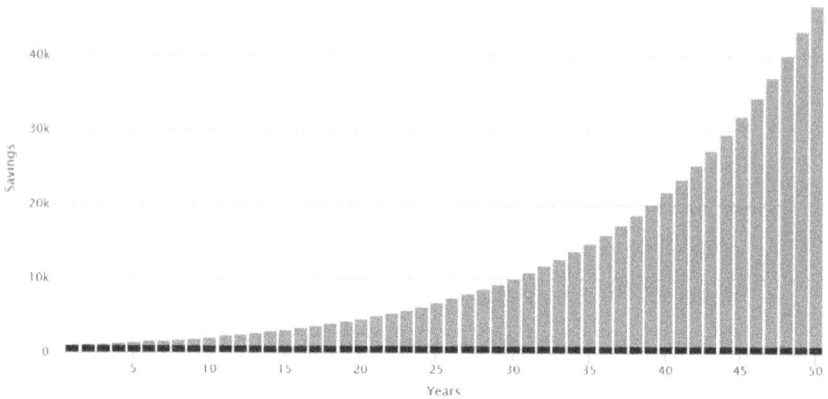

Results from moneysmart.gov.au/budgeting/compound-interest-calculator

This results in the interest being paid not only on the principle, but also on all the previously accrued interest. So, the interest each year would be as follows:

- Year 1: 8% of $1,000 = $80 (balance for Year 2 is $1,000 + $80 = $1,080).
- Year 2: 8% of $1,080 = $86.40 (balance for Year 3 is $1,080 + $86.40 = $1,166.40).
- Year 3: 8% of $1166.4 = $93.31 (balance for Year 4 is $1,166.4 + $93.31 = $1,259.71).
- Year 4: 8% of $1,259.71 = $100.78 (balance for Year 5 is $1,259.71 + $100.78 = $1,360.49).
- Year 5: 8% of $1,360.49 = $108.84 (balance for Year 6 is $1,360.49 + $108.84 = $1,469.33).

Basically, over time, the interest paid increases without any additional payments. Just like magic!

Alternatively, if we invested the initial deposit of one thousand dollars and made a small additional contribution of ten dollars each month, the balance would change from forty-six thousand dollars to nearly one hundred and twenty thousand dollars over fifty years. In other words, an additional six thousand dollars out of our pocket over fifty years would result in a balance increase of *seventy* thousand dollars!

This is the magic of compound interest!

Here is the breakdown for that in case you don't believe me!:

- Year 1: 8% of $1,000 = $80 (balance for Year 2 is $1,000 + $80 interest + $120 contribution or $10/month = $1,200).

- Year 2: 8% of $1,200 = $96 (balance for Year 3 is $1,200 + $96 + $120 = $1,416).

- Year 3: 8% of $1,416 = $113.28 (balance for Year 4 is $1,416 + $113.28 + $120 = $1,649.28).

- Year 4: 8% of $1,649.28 = $131.94 (balance for Year 5 is $1,649.28 + $131.94 + $120 = $1,901.22).

- Year 5: 8% of $1,901.22 = $152.10 (balance for Year 6 is $1901.22 + $152.10 + $120 = $2,173.32).

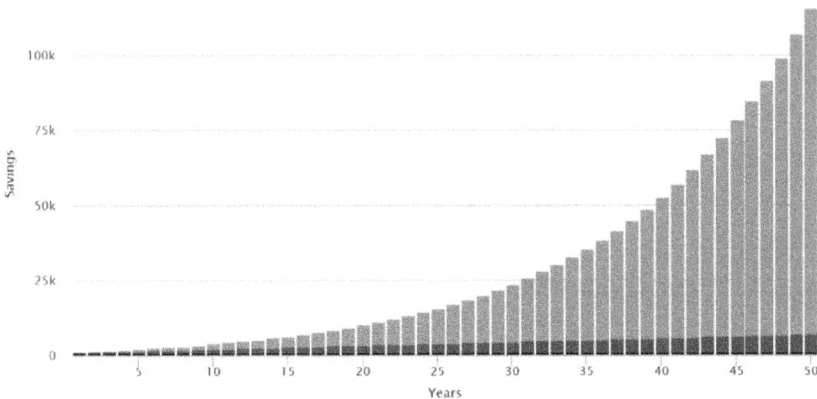

Even over five years and when only contributing six hundred dollars, the balance increases by over *seven hundred dollars* ($2,173 - $1,469).

To help explain compound interest to children, let's use the analogue of a tree (your initial investment) to grow a forest.

So, we start with one tree. Over time, it produces a seed (interest). If you plant that seed, over time it will grow into a tree. Now there are two trees that will produce two seeds. If planted, these two seeds will grow into two new trees—so you will have four trees. If you plant the four seeds that they produce, you will have eight trees.

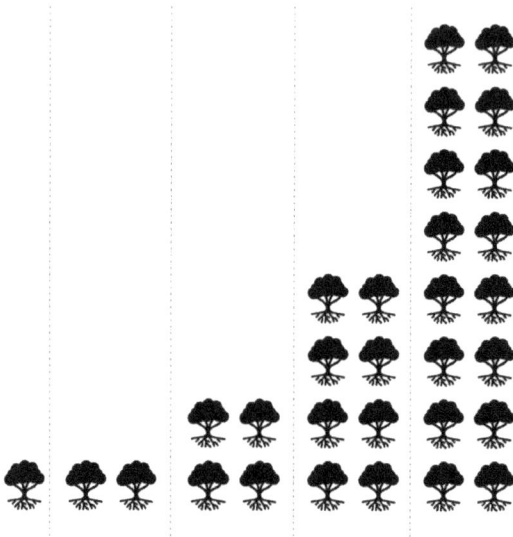

Trees take a long time to grow, so you need to be patient, but once the forest starts to grow, it will continue to multiply. If you then start to add some water (extra cash), it will grow even faster and produce even more seeds, resulting in the forest getting even larger.

With simple interest, only the original tree produces seeds. So instead of a forest of sixteen trees at this point, you would only have five.

To summarise, the sooner our children learn, earn, save, give, and invest, the more they will benefit from their personal finance in the future—and with a share portfolio, any dividend reinvestment can serve as additional contributions that will supercharge this compounding effect. We'll be going into this further in Chapter 7.

Action

Understanding personal finance and how to manage your money is not a set-and-forget task; it is a continual thinking process that involves understanding how we spend our money and why, setting up as many automated systems as possible (in turn taking human temptation away), reviewing these systems, and regularly taking action. It involves having savings goals and visualising the lifestyle you want—and then giving the possibility of this freedom and lifestyle to your children by teaching them how to become financially independent themselves.

This may not happen overnight, but it can happen if you're willing to take your time, continually learn, and take action.

Just think, wouldn't it have been good if you'd had these habits instilled in you at a young age so they were automatic by the time you reached adulthood and so you never had to worry about money as a result?

The following chapters will cover the successful ways of handling some basic money habits, including the Tooth Fairy, pocket money versus chores, saving, charities, and investing for the future.

Remember, don't look backwards, even if you think you currently don't have a good handle on your financial situation. Instead, focus on the future and develop your roadmap with your child. Start today, start small, and start together, and you'll quickly see that the processes and systems you set up for your children will form the foundation of their roadmap for financial independence.

You may be thinking that this is a lot of information to take on and that you're not sure whether your children are ready for this yet... so let me tell you a few stories to put your mind at ease.

My daughter's kindergarten teacher, Kylie, overheard a conversation between my daughter and a group of other four-year-olds about when their mums were going to pick them up. One child said, 'My mum has to work until really late, so I don't know when she's coming.' Another said, 'Mum said she was coming soon, but she has to work,' and my daughter said, 'Mum worked really hard when she was young, so she doesn't have to go to work now. She can work if she wants to, but she wants to spend time with me instead!'

When Kylie told me this, I was very surprised and happy. I couldn't recall talking to my four-year-old daughter about working hard early in life, but then again, children as young as four constantly overhear conversations and are sponges for information… and they also have memories like elephants.

My point is, you don't have to obsess over money or constantly talk about going to work in order to plant a seed in your kids. Rather, if you're having everyday positive conversations about what you spend and why, they will pick up on and take note of your habits.

Another positive example I would like to share about young children understanding the basics of personal finance is book clubs. Do you remember getting book club catalogues from school and spending hours looking at all the books and circling the ones you wanted? Well, my girls love books, and after going through and choosing the ones they wanted from the catalogue, my six-year-old came up to me and asked, 'Mum, if I buy this maze book for three dollars from my spending money, will you help me borrow the Kitticorn book from the library so I can see if I love it before spending my money on it, please?'

My six-year-old daughter is a natural spender! If we're going to the shops, she'll always bring her spending money in case there's something she wants, or if we haven't been to the shops for a while, she'll ask to be taken there so she can spend it. She's also very generous (as spenders usually are), and often spends her money on gifts for others. On the other hand, my four-year-old is a natural saver: she'll only spend money if the people around her are spending, such as buying ice cream or a lollipop from the canteen after swimming.

Whether our children are natural spenders or savers, as a parent, it's up to us to help our kids to balance out the two sides of spending and saving.

Key Takeaways

- Financial independence is having the means and passive income to decide how you spend your time.
- Having multiple sources of income will take you on the most direct route to financial independence.
- Goals (including financial independence) are about the results you want to achieve, but you need systems and processes in place in order to change behaviours into automatic habits to achieve those results.
- To gain confidence in taking action, you need a clear roadmap/plan to take you from where you are now to where you want to go, with clear goals and targets so you know what success looks like.
- The three key elements to gaining financial independence are:
  - An understanding of personal finance—so your children can have complete confidence in managing their finances, no

matter how little or much they have.

o Time—which is on your children's side. Starting young will give them the greatest chance of building wealth and happiness.

o Action—which is a requirement. Knowledge without action is just intent, so take small action steps regularly.

2

The Best Conversations You Can Have with Your Children

Something to remember to convey when having finance-related conversations is that it doesn't matter if you have more or less money than others, provided you're grateful for what you have, share it generously, and spend it wisely on things that make you happy.

Give a man a fish, and you will feed him for a day. Teach a man to fish, and you will feed him for a lifetime.

—LAO TZU

Okay, you now know that it is in your child's best interests to teach them about money—but where do you start with this? And how do you answer all their questions about your finances as they grow up—questions like, 'Are we rich?', 'Can you buy me this?' and 'Why can't I have this?'

This chapter will help guide you through having these seemingly difficult conversations about money; that is, how to answer your kids' questions openly and honestly while still using money to teach values such as gratitude, honesty, and perseverance.

This chapter does not aim to provide definite rules you *must* follow, but instead aims to provide guidelines for conversations that I've used before with my children so you can begin to build a framework and roadmap with your children's ultimate financial success in mind. We'll mainly cover the most common situations in which money-related conversations occur with your kids and how to use these as opportunities to teach your kids the financial values you want them to have.

I would like to share a story about my friend Nerida. By the time Nerida hit university, she'd never been responsible for her own money, nor had she ever heard her family discussing their finances; she'd always just assumed that money was either too terrible to talk about or was simply something only adults talked about in private, and thus that it was something to worry or argue about away from public spaces or listening ears.

Nerida is not alone in this experience: many people go through their childhoods without any exposure to money management... and when they leave home, they're thrown into the 'real world', where banks practically give away money through credit cards and personal loans without giving sufficient warning for the potential consequences, such as borrowing more than you can afford to pay back and having to pay back significantly more money than you borrowed due to the high interest rates of the loans.

Fortunately, Nerida had a roommate who'd been taught the basics and so could help her budget, pay rent, and buy groceries, but others aren't so lucky and get themselves into a lot of 'bad debt' early on in their life as a result. (We'll go into what I consider 'bad debt' in detail later, but essentially, 'bad debt' is borrowing money to purchase something that doesn't provide income, such as a car or some new clothes.)

The bottom line is, parents have the power to shape their children's relationships with money—and you need to start wielding your influence by having honest conversations with your kids so you can show them where money comes from (earning), how to set savings goals (saving), how to budget and spend wisely (spending), and how to be grateful for and share what they have (giving).

Sounds easy, right? So why doesn't everyone do this? Because people generally don't like to talk about money! And I've found that this tends to be due to several different reasons:

- Some believe they will raise money-grubbing, entitled children by talking about money. None of us want 'spoilt' children!

- Others don't like the negative emotions or feelings that arise when they talk about the money they have or how much they spend—or how much they *don't* have.

- For some, silence around money is simply their norm because of the society they and/or their parents grew up in. It wasn't socially acceptable to discuss money-related matters when they were growing up, so they continue not to.

Unfortunately, parents who have these fears often find it difficult to have open and honest conversations with their children about money. However, this book will help you to transform these beliefs and start viewing money positively so your children will grow up with a healthy relationship with money.

To address the first concern: if you use money to teach your children important values, you'll raise them to be the *opposite* of 'spoilt', even if you talk about it lots! For example, pocket money is a good opportunity to teach your children about working hard and the fact that they need to do their jobs to an agreed-upon standard in order for them to get paid. Pocket money is also about teaching patience: your children won't get everything they want straight away if they know they must earn in order to make purchases, but if their goal is important and will give them a lot of joy, they'll learn this delayed gratification is always worth the wait.

> *You can use pocket money to teach your children values. Hard work, perseverance, patience, and kindness are attributes that will see your children thriving in the world.*

As we've briefly mentioned, it's important to teach your children about giving and generosity. Spending is about enjoying the moment and having gratitude, while work is about perseverance—and both bases are covered through a pocket money system.

Something that may not be obvious to you in the moment but will greatly impact your kids later down the line is the fact that not being honest and open about money through healthy conversations is tantamount to you sheltering your children. Choosing silence over open conversation about money produces the idea that money is a problem and something to fear. And if you want your kids to obsess about something, treat it like a secret! Besides, they'll find a way to get the information they want in the end, and if this doesn't come directly from you, it may not be correct.

Values Taught Through Pocket Money

Earning
• Perseverance
• Determination

Saving
• Patience
• Gratification

Giving
• Kindness
• Generosity

Spending
• Happiness
• Gratitude

To summarise: children are sponges, absorbing whatever is around them, so positive conversations about money will produce a positive experience around money for them.

With that said, you will still need to expect the emotions that often arise around money, such as jealousy, tantrums, and disappointment, as well as happy times. I'll never forget how happy my daughter was when she finally saved enough money to buy the toy horse she wanted! She carried it all around the shopping centre, proudly showing it to everyone with a huge, cheesy grin on her face. It was the kind of smile that made strangers smile back at her!

Another thing to keep in mind with regards setting your kids up for financial independence is that you should never lie about money. When your children ask you to buy them something, don't say, 'We can't afford it,' or, 'I don't have any money,' if you don't want them to have it. They'll figure out that you aren't telling the truth, and if you keep brushing them off, they'll put their detective skills to the test and start looking in your wallet, handbag, or desk drawers to find the real answers! Instead, model sound principles and intentionally create teachable moments regarding money so your children can learn how to handle money. Don't obsess, but do make money part of everyday conversation. Every time you talk about money or answer one of your children's questions is an opportunity for you to teach them values and financial principles.

Below are some of the more common money questions parents get asked by their kids.

'Are We Rich?' or 'How Much Money Do You Make?'

While we want to try to answer our children honestly when we can, I've found that the best way to answer these questions is to ask them, 'Why do you ask?' in an encouraging voice. By doing this, you'll give yourself time to think about the most appropriate response, as well as to determine what the underlying question actually is. Have they heard something in the playground? Is it about having or buying a specific toy? Or understanding what homelessness means? Maybe they're asking out of fear after hearing an argument, and so need reassurance. Considering there'll more than likely be an underlying reason for them asking the question, giving your kid a dollar value will make no sense to them (not if they're a younger kid, anyway), as they don't have the relevant context to deduce what this means in a practical sense (or in relation to what they're really wondering). So, it's more important to find out what's on their minds and go from there.

Of course, you can be more open to older kids and explain some of your monthly costs versus your income. You can also include them in the budgeting process: for instance, if you make an extra fifty dollars one month, you can ask for their input on whether you should all go to the movies together or save it. A friend of mine has her high-school-aged daughter do all her money management for a four- to six-week period a few times a year to teach her this lesson, during which time her daughter pays all bills that are due, does the grocery shopping, and even helps decide whether she should work overtime that month—a trade-off between extra mother-daughter time or affording more things that month.

When your child asks you a question or for advice about money, remember that the absence of advice is often not the best advice. So, no silence and no lying, and make your home a safe place to ask questions—and remember to ask why they're asking every time! They may be asking or worrying about something entirely different to what their question implies on the surface of it.

'Why Does Mum/Dad Have to Go to Work?'

Explain that Mum/Dad has a job that pays them a salary, so Mum/Dad goes to work and gets a set amount of money each week or month in return. As a family, we then decide what to spend that money on each month. There are things we *need*, such as groceries, clothes, and gas/electric/water, and then there are things we *want*, such as sweets, going camping, or buying presents. We only have a set amount of money each month, so we must decide where to spend it or save it. To put this idea into practice, you can download the 'Needs vs Wants' activity sheet and complete this with your children at www.kidsfinance.com.au/resources. This will make this whole thing click into place for them.

'Can You Buy Me This Toy, Please?'

Instead of just saying, 'No,' or, 'I don't have the money,' you could use one of the following responses:

- 'No, that isn't something I want to spend my money on right now.' You can follow this up with, 'I can take a photo of it so that you can add it to your Christmas or birthday wish list?' Not purchasing straight away will help teach delayed gratification and patience. In a world of on-demand technology, this conveys the message that you shouldn't indulge in everything you want right now, especially if you don't need it.
- 'You almost have enough of your money to buy this. We will come back to purchase it then.' Setting savings goals and financial priorities (and sticking to them) will allow you to teach discipline and help your children to understand responsibility while providing guidance and direction. I will go into more detail about how to discourage 'impulse buying' later.

- 'No, we don't have money for that.' The significant difference here is in the words 'for that'. You teach self-control by not purchasing items you haven't planned to buy. This is an excellent lesson to teach. Explain that if you buy things that you don't have the money for, you'll go into debt, in turn costing more money—so instead, we save up and budget to purchase the items that we want. This teaches our children to live within their means.

- 'You can save up your pocket money and buy it yourself when you have enough.' Saving money carefully and planning to make deliberate, well-thought-out purchases will teach children discipline and keep them from making poor decisions. (Of course, to make this relevant to your child, you must implement the simple saving systems outlined in the following chapters.)

'How Much Money Does the Tooth Fairy Bring?'

When discussing with the Tooth Fairy, how much she might give to your child, remember the actual amount doesn't have to be the same each time. For example, the Tooth Fairy may give five dollars for the first tooth and then one dollar after that, or a different kind of coin for each tooth. Alternatively, it can be kept simple by giving a two-dollar coin for each tooth. Either way, it's good to have a conversation with your children about the Tooth Fairy before she comes so there aren't unrealistic expectations and subsequent disappointments.

A few examples of what the Tooth Fairy might do to make this time even more special are:

- A glass of water with the tooth replaced with shiny gold coins with glitter.
- Fairy dust or glitter leading to gold coins hidden in the room.

- A polished, super-shiny gold coin left on the bedside table.
- A unique gift, such as an animal tooth or a puzzle.

The first time the Tooth Fairy comes is exhilarating for children. It's something they will have looked forward to potentially more than Santa and the Easter Bunny coming, or their birthday—so make this memorable for your child but achievable for your family. I find getting my kids to place their tooth in a glass of water or container on their bedside table makes it a lot easier for the Tooth Fairy to see compared to under their pillow, which could wake them.

'Why Is That Person Homeless?' or 'Why Don't We Have As Much Money As [Someone Else]?'

Having difficult conversations about why some people have more than others will give your children perspective. I've been guilty of walking past a homeless person asking for money without giving them a second glance before, but now, I use this opportunity to talk to my daughters about the person's situation. We may give them a few dollars or stop and wish them luck, but the conversation between me and my daughter that follows is the most essential part of the exchange. It is important to reinforce that sometimes, things just happen that are out of our control, such as losing jobs due to COVID-19. This is why giving is imperative: so the person in question can have a community that cares and helps them get back on their feet, so that one day, they can do the same for others. Explain that life is not about how many material possessions you have: to be genuinely happy, you just need to be grateful for what you have, share it generously with others, and spend your money consciously on the things that make you happiest. Our children may not have all the toys they want, have visited all the places they want to go to, or have done all the fun things they want to, but they must recognise that there are a lot of children that aren't as fortunate as them: some don't get Christmas gifts or a cake for their birthday, or even some essential school needs.

> *The aim of this conversation is not to make our children feel guilty or entitled, but to make them thankful for what they have—and not just for the material possessions they have, but for living in a safe environment and being surrounded by people who love them.*

This is also a good point at which to bring up manners: manners are important, because when you say thank you, you show appreciation for who that person is and what they've done for you. It's a simple and effective way of showing love and respect and making them feel appreciated and special.

Manners can sometimes be delivered on autopilot, so encourage your children to stop and look the person in the eyes when saying thank you. In this way, they can better acknowledge how important that person is and appreciate the action. And a heartfelt thank-you is always rewarded with a smile!

Here are some gratitude activities you can complete with your children:

1. Each time your child says thank you to someone, ask them to check to see if the person smiled back. This will encourage them to use a clear voice, look at the person, and smile when saying thank you.

2. As a family, list all the people and things you are thankful for. For example, my family and I often discuss before dinner each night one person or event that made us smile or we were grateful for today.

3. At Christmas time, wrap up a toy in your house that is no longer used and donate it to a Christmas appeal through a local charity.

'Do You Give Money to Other People?'

The best way to answer this question is by saying 'yes', and then doing so! You don't have to give much; this could just be a two-dollar raffle ticket for a charity, old clothes (to a charity shop), or a monthly charity donation. We personally pick a new charity every three to six months to ensure there is continual conversation around giving and helping those in need. Modelling consistent generosity and making sure your kids participate in this will encourage their joy of giving and instil generosity in them at an early age.

'I Wanted to Buy This Shirt/Toy/Book, But I Didn't Bring My Money. Can You Buy It?'

When we want to buy things we hadn't planned on purchasing, this is referred to as 'impulse buying'. Generally, I encourage my kids to wait for at least twenty-four hours before making any big purchases, especially if it's something they've only just seen for the first time and decided they want. Sometimes, I take a photo of it and then promise to bring them back to the shop for it at another time. Nine times out of ten, they forget about it or find something else they want instead. If it's the last of a specific item, we ask the person behind the counter to hold it for us, and most shops will do this for twenty-four to forty-eight hours.

Speaking of impulse buying: impulse buying is driven by emotions and happens when someone buys something without planning to or fully considering the consequences of doing so. The product in question can be something small, like a chocolate bar at the checkout, or as big as a new TV at a seventy percent off sale.

Large items bought on impulse could cause financial tension if the money spent was intended for something else, such as if children save for a special toy, see and purchase something else, and then feel disappointed when they can't buy the other thing they'd saved for.

Some people like to go shopping when they're sad or stressed to feel better, and once this becomes a habit, it's hard to break. As a parent, you never want to see your children sad or disappointed about something, and so when this happens, it's tempting to say, 'Will an ice cream or new toy make it better?' I'm not saying you can't buy them treats, but you don't always want to associate spending money and buying treats with happiness, so just be conscious of this connection that you're creating between negative feelings and impulse buying as a remedy.

Section Activities

Your activities for this chapter are:

- ☐ If you haven't already done so, download the 'Needs vs Wants' worksheet from www.kidsfinance.com.au/resources so your kids can begin identifying what they need vs what they want. Work through this with your children so they understand that money is still needed for the basic needs such as food and shelter, and in order to be 'wealthy' instead 'rich', we need to prioritise living within our means and planning for the future.

- ☐ In the same vein, download 'Top 10 Tips to Stop Impulse Buying' from www.kidsfinance.com.au/resources, and the next time you are in a shop and want to buy something you hadn't planned to, talk with your child about waiting for twenty-four hours before making any impulse purchases.

- ☐ Next time you're tempted to cheer your child up with treats, first acknowledge they are feeling sad, injured, or disappointed, and then change the topic to something else once they have processed their emotions... and *then* suggest an ice cream or treat.

Key Takeaways

- Remember that money is a teaching tool that uses the value of a dollar to instil positive traits in our children.
- Children model the behaviour they see, so they'll save as you do, spend as you do, and give as you do. You don't have to be perfect; just talk about your choices while shopping with your children.
- You influence your children's thinking and decision-making abilities by being open and having regular conversations about money.
- No lying, no silence, and make home a safe place to ask questions—but where appropriate, ask why they are asking before giving them an answer.

3

Earning

Have you ever wondered why some children simply put a toy back on the shelf and say, 'Okay, Mum,' when told they can't have it, while others have a complete meltdown?

No, this isn't down to luck. It's down to parenting.

While children often learn well by watching and modelling behaviour, they often learn lessons quicker by making the decisions (and mistakes) themselves.

Now, most financial transactions these days involve 'invisible money', such as online transfers and card payments, so there's not a whole lot of physical cash used anymore. For this reason, we should encourage children to take responsibility for a small amount of physical money so they can start to understand the nature of exchanging money in a largely cash-free world. It's better for our children to misspend six dollars when they're young than sixty thousand dollars as an adult!

With this in mind, this chapter will explain how to introduce pocket money and use it to teach valuable lessons.

My family owned a farm while I was growing up, and during my childhood and adolescent years, it was instilled in me that working on the farm and doing chores wasn't optional: the cows *must* be milked and the calves *must* be fed every day, even before opening Christmas presents. Of course, there were often arguments about whose turn it was to do each job among my siblings and I, but this still created a work ethic in us that I'm very grateful for.

My husband also has a strong work ethic, built from working numerous part-time jobs. This started in primary school in the form of mowing neighbours' lawns, and turned into doing odd jobs within the community he lived in and working part-time during university.

I want that same work ethic ingrained in our children. The problem is that we don't live on a farm, nor do we live in a small community where everyone knows each other—meaning often, it's not safe for young kids to be out by themselves until after dark anymore. So, how do we give our children the experience to learn and understand the importance of working hard and being rewarded financially?

I have found the best way to introduce young children to this concept is to get your children to work in a safe environment—your home—and then, eventually, close friends' and neighbours' houses, until they're old enough to obtain a part-time job independently. After all, for children to appreciate the value of money, they need to have their *own* money and make their *own* decisions, as this will allow them to learn the lessons that result from their choices.

There are many ways for children to earn money, and the most common approach to this is pocket money. This takes many different forms in different families: some give twenty cents for every 'chore' the child does every day; others provide a set amount to their kids every week, no matter what; some don't give any pocket money at all and just give their kids a list of chores they expect to be done every week.

One of the main reasons why some parents *don't* give pocket money is because they don't think children should be rewarded for or paid to help around the house: being part of a family means you contribute to the household (and do chores), end of story. With our family, there is a difference between helping to do what *needs* doing (housework) and having the opportunity to do additional paid work (jobs). So, I want to clarify that when I refer to pocket money, I'm referring to the money paid to the children of the household for doing a specific job, not for doing the 'chores' that contribute to the household, such as setting the table, putting dishes in the sink, or throwing dirty clothes in the laundry basket. These are daily expectations in our family, just like having a bath or shower or brushing our teeth before bed, because this teaches social and family responsibility and gives a good sense of accomplishment—not to mention the fact that it helps them to actually learn practical skills. The earlier you start assigning household tasks, the earlier these will become a habit. The checklist of tasks before school, such as packing bags, cleaning teeth, and putting on sunscreen, is a reminder of expectations, not a list of paid jobs. So, when I talk about giving pocket money, I mean that I recommend giving your children the opportunity to do specific jobs for money in *addition* to these standard, routine household chores that they *don't* get money for.

While these additional jobs are, of course, likely to be done quicker, easier, and to a higher standard if you do them yourself, it's essential to remember that teaching our children to work doesn't just benefit us; it gives our children a sense of accomplishment and the tools to succeed as an adult. For example, learning to hang clothes out correctly will keep clothes in the correct shape and help them to last longer. Also, an appreciation of a clean, well-organised room will help during busy periods.

One rule to bear in mind with this: choose jobs for pocket money that do not *need* to be completed that day. It's important to adhere to this rule, since if you choose a daily task that has to be done no matter what (such as feeding the dog) and your children don't do it, you, as a parent, must do it for them—and unfortunately, this can reinforce the belief that if they don't want to work, there will always be someone else who will do it for them. Now, on occasion, this can't be helped: they may have a busy weekend camping, or they may need to study for an exam, and so they haven't put the wheelie bin out that week, and during these times, it's okay to do their job(s) for them, provided this doesn't happen all the time. Generally speaking, though, things don't often come free in life, and you, as parents, won't always be there to give your children everything they want and need. So, this means children must learn to *earn* luxuries in life so they don't get a nasty surprise when they're not being financially supported by you anymore. Therefore, when setting up the pocket money system, it's pivotal that they don't get paid if they don't do the work.

One week, one of my daughters decided that she didn't want to do any of her jobs. This decision was fine—after all, it's her choice—and it worked well in creating a teachable moment, as her sister, who *did* do her jobs that week and thus received her pocket money, spent hers on lollipops and didn't share any with her sister. This resulted in a negative experience that she still remembers. No work = no pay!

Another advantage of your children doing weekly jobs such as cleaning their room is that if they *don't* do it, this doesn't affect anyone else except them and it'll probably take them twice as long to do it next time. For example, one of my daughters loves making craft projects, and so her room always has scissors and cut up bits of paper all over the floor. However, after the first week of having 'clean your room' on her job list and spending over an hour picking up every piece of paper by hand, she immediately started to use her bin while doing crafts!

This lasted a few weeks until we changed jobs (we keep the same three jobs for four weeks), and then the bad habit returned.

This was a good reminder for us to celebrate the small wins and not expect a permanent change after only a few weeks. Unfortunately, we can't just set a few jobs and give our children some money once a week in return and be done with it. Creating such momentum is excellent, but we need to be realistic with our expectations, and replacing habits with new ones takes time. And this makes sense, as teaching your children about finances is a journey.

Another reason why I'm a fan of pocket money is that it teaches children patience. Most things today are readily available on-demand, such as TV shows and the Internet, but children being made to wait to collect their weekly pocket money and buy fun things means they learn to be patient in an otherwise-'instantaneous' world. In addition, waiting is associated with good financial habits in adulthood, especially in relation to avoiding the bad debt acquired from 'needing' everything straight away, and so teaching our children to wait actually forms a big part of the overall goal.

With practice and through a pocket money system, kids can develop the kind of restraint that will consistently keep them out of trouble while still allowing them to spend on things that bring them joy.

As the kids have gotten older, I've introduced more advanced concepts to our pocket money system, such as interest and getting a loan or cash advance on the following week's pocket money. For example, my six-year-old daughter once borrowed one dollar from her younger sister to buy a lollipop, and then had to pay one dollar and twenty cents back when she received her pocket money the following week. As a result, she isn't as keen to borrow money anymore!

Section Activities

Before you go any further, here are some tasks for teaching this lesson:
- ☐ Make a list of non-negotiable household chores expectations and don't include them as paid jobs.
- ☐ No system fits everyone perfectly, so modify what you've learned in this chapter to suit your family—and stick to it!

So, how do we implement a sustainable pocket money system?

Below, I'll describe the pocket money system we personally have implemented. This won't necessarily suit everyone, so feel free to adapt it to your needs. However, you *do* need to stick to whatever you choose.

Giving pocket money is a commitment, so don't start until you're ready. After all, you wouldn't take on an employee at work unless you intended to pay them every week, fortnight, or month, and the same applies to giving pocket money: it's compensation for doing a job—and doing it well and on time.

Step 1: Choose the Jobs

We try to make these jobs as straightforward as possible. In my family, each child has three jobs to be done per week, and each job takes less than fifteen minutes to complete. They can be done at any time during the week, but must be done by payday. In our case, this is Thursday, meaning our children must have completed their jobs by Thursday afternoon.

Here is a guide to choosing the jobs:

- Make the job age appropriate. Children should be able to do most of it themselves. You may need to assist your younger children to start with, but it is the act of doing the job that's important, not necessarily the quality of the job (until they get a bit older).
- Choose weekly jobs, not daily jobs. Have you ever successfully kept track of a daily job list? I remember trying a stickers-on-a-whiteboard approach once. It was very time consuming and confusing, as I couldn't remember if the children had done the task that day or the day before. Did they only do it five times, or seven? To avoid this confusion, I recommend keeping it simple by assigning each job to be done once per week.
- Keep it fun. You could allocate time during the weekend where everyone does jobs simultaneously with fun music in the background, or where they help each other complete their tasks (e.g., cleaning their rooms) quicker. You could even make it part of a game.

Below is a list of a few jobs you may consider for kids aged eight and under. A more comprehensive list can be found at www.kidsfinance.com.au/ resources, but to get you started, these could be:

- Cleaning their room.
- Tidying the play area (picking up toys).
- Sorting the laundry.
- Sweeping the floor.

Jobs that your children can complete once a week are ideal. However, you may want to introduce them to some more challenging jobs through pocket money before they become 'chores'. An example of this is emptying the dishwasher: it might be too much to expect a six-year-old to stack and/or unload a dishwasher every day, but you may decide to include it as a weekly job on the weekend, when you aren't as busy and can supervise. By spending time teaching your children to do the work properly when they are young, they'll know how to stack a dishwasher correctly when they're older and it is considered part of routine housework.

For eight- to fourteen-year-olds, jobs could include (though again, head over to the list at www.kidsfinance.com.au/resources for more ideas!):

- Gardening and yard work.
- Cleaning the toilets and/or bathrooms.
- Washing the dog.
- Cleaning the back deck.

How long you should keep your kids doing the same jobs for will depend on the routine and personality of your family. Some people like variety and operate best when living week to week; others prefer structure and knowing what to expect in advance.

What works for our family is keeping the same three jobs for each child for four to five weeks. I have found that anything less is hard to track; I spent more time organising the job lists and explaining each job than it took the children to do the jobs! Plus, having the opportunity to change jobs every month stopped the children from losing interest. For example, they may dislike cleaning out the car, but they're motivated to do it anyway because they know they only have to do it for a few weeks.

We sit together as a collective and discuss what went well and decide on new jobs approximately once a month. Generally, I choose one, they choose one, and we jointly agree on the third, but the rule is we all must agree on the final list of three. (Trust me, there's no point in putting something they'll ultimately refuse to do on the job list. It'll make the process so much harder!)

You can keep some of the jobs the same month to month, or change one or all of them as often as you and your kids like.

As an example, I'm a big fan of the task 'cleaning your room', as I like my kids to start the week with a clean room, and so I quite often include this in their list of jobs for a few months at a time.

Notably, throughout this process, it's important to keep expectations clear and positive. If you expect your children to complete a job, they'll need to know where all the cleaning products or supplies (e.g., brooms; wipes) are stored, which might mean you having to do the job with them the first time round or provide photo or written instructions of what they should do. When the children are older, they'll need to follow instructions from their boss at work (often independently or in a written form), so it's often a good idea to start introducing written 'work instructions' for later primary-school-age children.

For example, for cleaning the deck, the steps might be:

1. Get the hose and broom ready on the deck.
2. Find some old towels and put them near the doorway.
3. Remove or put away anything that doesn't belong on the deck.
4. Stack the chairs and move the furniture to the side.
5. Hose the deck and scrub it with a broom.
6. Put the hose and broom away and wipe off any extra water on the deck with an old towel.

7. Hang up the towel to dry.
8. Put the furniture back.

After the job is complete, check to see if it was done correctly. Remember, pocket money is not only for doing a job, but also for doing it *right*. If it's not quite right, you shouldn't redo the job in front of younger children. Instead, give them praise but then constructively provide them with some help. For example, 'The lounge rugs look good. Let me show you a trick for how I get the dirt from under the couch or at the edges.'

Step 2: Record When the Job is Complete

For some, one of the greatest satisfactions of doing work is the feeling of accomplishment that comes from completing it. Therefore, I recommend that you have a printed list of the jobs to be completed each week and stick it to the fridge or somewhere similarly visible, and then encourage your children to give it a tick as soon as the job has been finished and checked.

Here is an example of what we have on the fridge. I put it inside a clear magnetic photo frame and use a whiteboard marker to check each box off.

On payday, I take this off the fridge, sit with the girls, and discuss how many jobs they've done and how much money they will have earned this week.

This brings us to the next point: how much pocket money should you give?

	WEEK 1	WEEK 2	WEEK 3	WEEK 4
Empty Dishwasher				
Tidy Play Area				
Vacuum Lounge				

Step 3: Decide the Amount of Money to Pay

Every family's circumstances are different, but the key here is to be consistent. You also need to give your kids enough money where they can watch their funds grow *and* have enough to save and buy the things they want, but not too much so they have too many choices and unrealistic expectations.

One approach might be to have a list of jobs and decide on an amount that should be paid for each job depending on its value. For instance, putting laundry away might be two dollars, while washing the car is five dollars. This approach tends to work well for older children, who understand the value of money and choice.

The alternative method is the one we use for our younger children, where they have three jobs to do each week for a set amount of money. All these jobs are paid equally, and they have a maximum amount they can earn based on their age. I've found that between fifty cents to one dollar a week per year in age is an excellent start. For example, my six-year-old earns six dollars a week if she does all three jobs, but if she only does two out of three jobs, she's only paid two-thirds of the original amount (four dollars). Meanwhile, my four-year-old would be paid four dollars a week for doing all three jobs.

I find this approach works well, as they get a 'pay rise' each year—which makes sense, as the level of service you expect from each job also gets higher as they get older (e.g., cleaning a wheelie bin with a hose for younger kids and cleaning with a hose and chemicals for older kids).

Regardless of which approach you choose, starting to give your children pocket money is a commitment, and it needs to be sustainable. It doesn't matter whether you pay them fifty cents per year in age or two dollars per year in age, so long as it's sustainable for you and your family.

Step 4: Pay at the Same Time Every Week

You'll probably have to remind your children to do their jobs each week until they become a habit. The critical lesson here is to be very clear that they will only get paid if they do the job.

You should also be sure to pay your children at the same time each week. Make sure you have the correct amount of money to give to your child each week on the chosen day. It doesn't matter when you give your kids their pocket money so long as it's at the same time each week; don't do this, and your kids won't know by what day their jobs need to be done. A job list on the fridge is helpful to check whether their jobs are complete before handing over their pocket money.

Okay, now we have our approach in place, we may wonder: where should pocket money be stored? Should it be stored in bank accounts?

My answer to this is no, their pocket money shouldn't be put in a bank account (although we will go into bank accounts and investment options later). For now, an excellent alternative way to track and store pocket money is in clear containers (such as old peanut butter or vegemite jars) or clear pencil-case-type pouches so your kids can physically see their balance increasing.

We personally divide money into three plastic containers: 'save', 'give', and 'spend'. This introduces the idea that some money is for spending now, some is for giving to others, and some is for saving for something we want or need later.

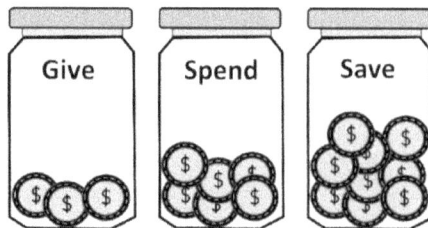

The 'save' container is for—you guessed it!—saving, for something recreational. This could be a special toy, or something more significant. Again, make sure the goals are achievable. I've found that around four to six weeks is the sweet spot for kids to wait before using their 'saving' money (young children tend to lose interest after that).

In our household, fifty percent of total pocket money goes into savings. My six-year-old daughter receives six dollars per week if she completes all three jobs, so three dollars per week goes into her saving container.

The 'give' container, meanwhile, is there to introduce the concept of sharing. Children can use this money to buy small presents for friends or fresh flowers for strangers, and as the children get older, they can choose to give money to a charity. (Tip: Select a charity that mails out receipts and a thank-you, as children love receiving letters!) It's good to donate every three to six months, or when the jar is full, whichever comes first. Even a small child can understand that the more money they put into the 'giving' container, the more they can help. In our case, one coin (one dollar) goes into the giving jar each week.

Finally, the 'spend' container is for just that: spending. So, encourage your children to spend on show rides, toys, tuckshop... anything that makes them smile! Children will only genuinely learn the lesson if *they* are the ones making the decision, so don't judge their choices; let them decide how they want to spend their pocket money.

> When sorting and allocating pocket money, the message to give is, 'Always pay your future yourself first, give something to make others smile, and then spend the rest on things that make you smile.'

I've also found it helpful to have a whiteboard explaining to my six-year-old how much money goes into her 'save', 'spend', and 'give' containers based on how many jobs she's done that week. It's also a good idea to use this to add up how much is in her savings each week and how much more she needs to save to purchase her chosen product or experience. An example of what we use is below.

	EMMA = 6	GEORGIA = 4
Number of Jobs	2/3	3/3
Extra Jobs	0	0
Total for This Week	$4	$4
Savings (50%)	$2	$2
Current Saving Total (Towards Savings Goal)	$15 ($35)	$10.50 ($25)
Giving	$0.50	$0.50
Spending (Total Minus 'Saving' and 'Giving')	$1.50	$1.50
Current Spending Total	$1.50	$4.50

What about birthday money or money given as a gift, you ask?

In my eyes, this money shouldn't be considered part of the pocket money system, and should instead either be spent on something straight away (as intended) or put into an online savings account to be put towards large items.

Having Multiple Sources of Income from Different Assets

So, are there other ways for kids to earn money besides the job ideas listed above?

Indeed, there are. In fact, one of the key lessons I want my daughters to learn early is that you shouldn't rely on just one source of income. Having multiple sources of income means that when one income source is underperforming, the others can buffer against this by providing additional income/security. For example, there will be no income from your salary if you lose your job, no income from investment properties if there is an oversupply of houses, and no income from dividends if the stock market crashes—so, to be truly financially independent, having numerous assets which produce different sources of income is vital.

To help put this into context, below is an example of how financial independence is achieved through different funding sources for *adults* (we will go into what this looks like for children soon).

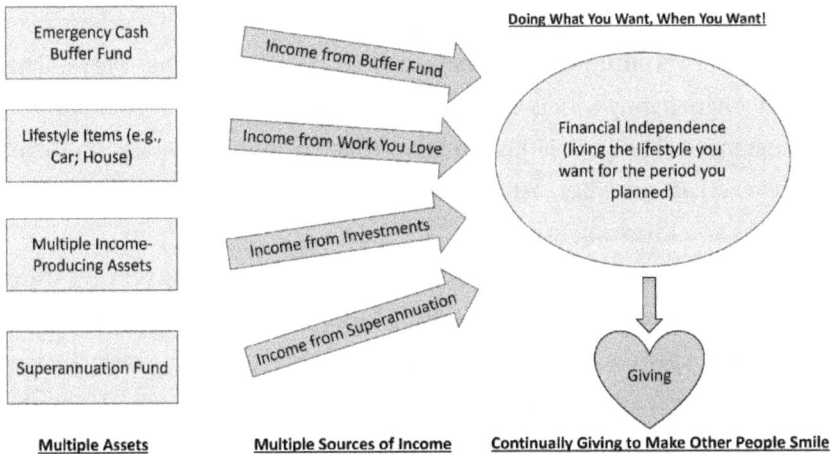

| Multiple Assets | Multiple Sources of Income | Continually Giving to Make Other People Smile |

The first asset one should look to acquire is a 'buffer' fund—one of the most crucial steps. Essentially, this is a cash account with enough money to cover living expenses in the unlikely scenario that you lose your main source of income. After all, life happens, and there might be a situation in which you need to access money quickly—for example, you may need to access your savings for medical emergencies, or use them as a bond so you can move into your first rental—and if you don't have any money available for these things, you'll end up needing to take out a loan from the bank, which may result in you acquiring debt and paying high interest.

Another possibility is you having money invested in the stock market and the stock market crashing, or having money invested in property and property prices going down, meaning you now need to realise your loss by selling at a non-optimal time (i.e., at a low price) to access your funds. (Though remember, even if the property or stock market goes down, it doesn't need to affect you until you sell.)

It is perfectly okay to use the money in your buffer account, should a critical moment arise; the only guideline here is that you must top up the buffer fund back to the desired level before investing or before making any new lifestyle purchases once you have dipped into it. Some people are happy having a three-month supply of savings in this account, while others may not sleep very well unless they have at least twelve months' worth. The amount you're happy with is up to you, and largely depends on your family's circumstances. The goal is just to have this account at the desired level (whatever that may be) *before* you put all your savings into lifestyle purchases and investing in assets.

In other words, there needs to be a balance between saving for the future and enjoying your life in the present. (To lead from this, Chapter 6 will detail some spending lessons to teach to your children, such as the difference between a want and a need and the appropriate use of a credit card so they can enjoy the lifestyle they live today.)

Another set of assets is your investments. Purchasing quality assets will give you an income in the future. In fact, investments should steadily increase in value over time (at a rate that you are comfortable with). Remember, investments don't necessarily increase every week, month, or year; there will be times when they decrease in value. However, they should (if history is anything to go off!) increase steadily over the longer term. The benefit of introducing your children to investments is the magical effect of time and compound interest. Chapter 7 will give you a few examples of how to start investing both for yourself and your children so you can begin putting this into practice.

The last asset (or future source of income) is the money that goes into your retirement fund. In Australia, this is called superannuation, but is known as a 401K in the U.S., and your employer pays this into a fund of your choice. This can be accessed as a funding source sometime in your sixties, though exactly when this is will be dependent on the rules set by the current government. We'll go into more detail about choosing superannuation (also known as a superfund) and the advantages and disadvantages of contributing additional funds to this in Chapter 8.

Superannuation is considered the icing on the financial independence cake, the 'layers' of which being the other main sources of income you have generated over time. Accordingly, it is essential to teach your children about this and help them to set up an appropriate retirement account *before* they start their first part-time job.

Finally, yet another (often overlooked) important aspect of being financially independent is giving. It doesn't matter how much money you have or the number of material things you possess; the lesson is to give what you can. There are some examples of this in Chapter 5 that will help your children to maintain these instinctive traits well into their adulthood.

The idea of these different sources of income is that over time, the amount of money you gain from your assets will become more extensive, and once this is the case, you can rely on your salary much less for living expenses... which means you can spend less time working and more time doing what you love.

Lucky for us parents, the concept of having multiple sources of income can be introduced from an early age, and the following should form a good starting point for you!

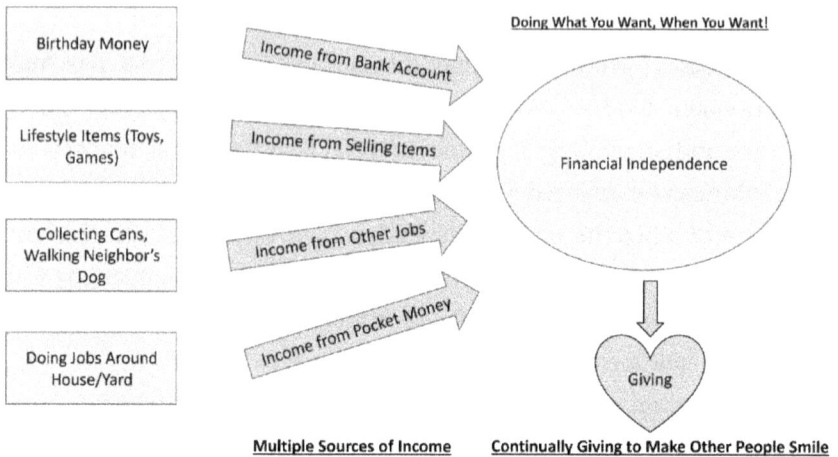

| Birthday Money | | Doing What You Want, When You Want! |

Income from Bank Account

Income from Selling Items

Financial Independence

Income from Other Jobs

Income from Pocket Money

Giving

Multiple Sources of Income   **Continually Giving to Make Other People Smile**

For children, these multiple sources of income can be:

- Interest from money in bank account. We will go through in detail later how and when to open bank accounts for your children.
- Selling old toys. Every six months, we go through the house and declutter any toys, appliances, furniture, books, or clothes that we no longer need or want as a family. We then put them into three piles:
  - First is 'recycle' (e.g., by taking a photo of all your child's artwork and making an online artbook before physically recycling the original pieces).
  - The second is 'give away', which is for toys and clothes that are to be taken to the op/charity shop for children who don't have many possessions. Make sure your child comes with you and physically hands over their belongings if you choose to do this. You may also wish to bring some money from their container so they can purchase something second-hand, and explain that the money is to help the charity while you're there.
  - The third pile is 'sell', for items which are in near-new condition. Help your child to list these items on Gumtree or the marketplace by looking at how much it costs new and how

many similar second-hand items are for sale, and pricing accordingly. It's good to expose little kids to the concept of buying and selling second-hand goods so that when they're looking to purchase something new, you can look together at how much a brand-new one costs compared to a second-hand one. Plus, with the money they save from purchasing the latter, there might be an additional item they could buy!

- Collecting and recycling cans and plastic bottles. They can gather these from around the house, place them into specific bins, and even ask neighbours or friends if they could put a recycling container in their home. Yes, this means you'll need to load cans in your car and drive them to the recycling centre every so often, but your children will still be collecting the bins when they're full and organising a suitable time to take them to the recycling centre.
- Doing odd jobs for friends or neighbours, or other tasks at home outside of their pocket money jobs. For example, older children can mow lawns, do other yard work, wash cars, walk pets, or clean windows.
- Making things to sell at the markets, such as birthday cards or hair ties/scrunches.
- If the children enjoy doing the work, they could create a weekend side-business—a potential win-win if some older adults without close family would appreciate the company of the children and their windows being washed.

For this to be successful, these jobs also need to be agreed upon and listed and expectations regarding them outlined (just like with their pocket money jobs). You'll also need an agreement regarding the amount they are to be paid and how regularly the tasks are to be performed. For example, you might outline that your children can clean the lounge room windows once a month for ten dollars. Otherwise, they might want to clean the same windows every day and expect ten dollars each time.

The income from these additional tasks can also be divided across three containers, or, alternatively, this would be a good time to introduce their first bank account. We described this bank account as their long-term savings (essentially, it is their first buffer account), which is used for saving for their future selves (i.e., a car, phone, etc.).

From the age of fourteen, you should encourage your children to get out and about and find experience working for someone else, either by starting their own business (such as babysitting or dog walking) or by working at a local store (like Coles or McDonald's). Remember you will probably need to be their taxi service for this, so pick an employment location that suits the family—maybe a fifteen-kilometre radius from home—and encourage them to ride their bike for any weekend shifts.

Ultimately, the pocket money system is a win-win for everyone involved: you'll be saving money (as it will no longer be you who pays for the lollipops or ice creams after swimming lessons or the tuckshop treats at school), and your children will be paying more consideration to whether they would prefer to buy a lolly each week or go without for a few weeks and then buy an ice cream after their swimming lesson. I know for my kids, figuring out that a lollipop is only fifty cents (meaning they could buy that *and* get a slushie at the tuckshop the next day) was a gratifying experience for them.

And to give you some more inspiration, my nieces and nephew, who are a bit older, often visit their grandparents after school while their parents work, and they have earned a lot of money both for themselves and their grandparents by:

1. Doing odd jobs that can be time consuming and disliked by their grandparents, such as window-washing.
2. Cleaning, sorting, and selling all sorts of old 'treasure' which is no longer needed or wanted and would otherwise just sit in the shed, such as an old treadmill, furniture, vases, cake tins, and puzzles.

In our family, this has been a win-win for both parties: the children earn extra money doing the work, their grandparents get to declutter, and the children learn valuable lessons and experience a sense of accomplishment. In addition, the children can experience a good sort of tiredness as a result and something to feel good about instead of the kind of lethargy that comes from too much time spent on a computer game or iPad. It makes them feel confident that they can do anything—and isn't that priceless?

Although I have mentioned that starting pocket money is a commitment, don't get discouraged if your children want a break from doing 'jobs' and getting paid. I have found that this happens when they either aren't motivated or are getting what they want from other sources. For example: just after Christmas or their birthday, they have everything they want, so they may not be motivated to save (Chapter 4 will go through the importance of goal setting), or we, as the parents, might have unconsciously gone back to buying them the odd lollipop as a reward or giving tuckshop money (because we haven't been grocery shopping), so they aren't motivated to earn their own money.

Alternatively, they might be starting to get an entrepreneurial spirit and may be working out ways to earn more money for doing less 'work'. For example, my daughters stopped doing their jobs for a while after my husband agreed to pay them twenty dollars if they did a daily sit-up challenge with him.

Whatever the reason, taking a break from jobs and pocket money is fine, especially if it is not a rewarding experience for your child. Take a break, reset, and look at the next steps.

To summarise: teaching your child about money and how to work is *your responsibility*. This isn't going to happen at school or with their friends. The direction they take in life and whether they end up being financially responsible when they're adults starts with you. This won't always be easy, but the bottom line is that you're their biggest supporter and best teacher, and so a solid foundation of hard work and a good work ethic will only be developed if you, as their parent or carer, get involved and teach them how and why work matters.

Section Activities

I recommend you read the following chapters on saving and spending before you sit down with children and discuss the pocket list system, but in the meantime, you can:

- ☐ Write down a list of potential jobs you want your children to do and have this ready to discuss with them.
- ☐ Think about how you'll pick between these jobs. In my family, to start with, I chose one, the children chose one, and we all agreed on the third. You may wish to select all three or let your children choose all three; it's up to you.
- ☐ Think about how long you'd like to wait before changing the jobs. You could suggest a fortnight, or the four to five weeks that I use, and see how it goes. Either way, make sure you're clear on the date on which you'll agree to revise jobs.
- ☐ Determine how much pocket money to give. I recommend having a discussion with your partner about this before you do it with the kids, just so you can be super-clear about what is and is not feasible for you as a family.
- ☐ Have plastic containers or clear pouches ready to store pocket money. Each child will need three containers: one for saving, one for giving, and one for spending. You could also have some stickers or ribbons ready to help decorate these when you give them to the children!
- ☐ Look around the house and determine what could be sold on Gumtree or the marketplace.

Key Takeaways

- Having your children earn their own money and make decisions using it will help them to appreciate the value of hard work and determination. It will also empower them to make informed choices regarding their finances.
- Starting a weekly pocket money arrangement is a commitment. Don't start until you are ready and this is sustainable for you.
- No work, no pay! It's important for your kids to know that money must be earned. Do the work, and you'll get paid. Don't work, and you won't get paid.
- Introduce the concept of multiple sources of income early and explain that having different sources of income allows for more options in the future.
- If your kids don't learn the value of work when they're young, it'll be more difficult for them to learn this when they're adults. Your children may not like every aspect of this system at the time (parenting isn't easy!), but they *will* thank you for it later, and that's what counts.

4

Saving

'*Paying myself first' was one of the best strategies I implemented, and was fundamental for me setting up regular savings and getting financially ahead. It is also critical to have the mindset that your future self is important, and this mindset starts when you are young.*

You can make a million excuses, or you can make a million dollars.

—UNKNOWN

As mentioned previously, I am an engineer, and if you've met any engineers before, you probably will have noticed that we typically like spreadsheets, to-do lists, measuring progress, and Key Performance Indices (KPIs). This is because it was drilled into us at university and our jobs that you focus on what you measure, and you make improvements on what you focus on. So, when it came to saving, I (at the very start of my journey) had an elaborate plan: first, I'd get paid in one account and then transfer a certain amount of that to a different bank account for my weekly spending. I would then move some money towards my monthly bills (e.g., rent and electricity), some to my credit card, some to my holiday fund, and then some to the wedding and funeral fund.

This list went on and on.

I also bought, sold, and tracked various shares regularly, and had investments in nine different managed funds.

The plan looked great on paper, and it projected I would be a millionaire by the time I was thirty—but unfortunately, the projected results just... weren't happening.

The problem wasn't with my calculations, nor was it that I didn't want to be a millionaire. What was holding me back was my ability to execute such a complicated plan every month. It had *way* too many manual steps for me to keep track of, and was thus too time consuming. Instead, I needed a good money management strategy that ran smoothly without me needing to think about it all the time; a strategy that would allow me to fall asleep at night without financial stress.

After this revelation, I read many books and talked to many people about how they managed their money, and my two most remarkable takeaways were: maximise simplicity, and remove temptation. In other words, I learned that you'll give yourself the best chance of successfully managing your money if you implement a simplified, streamlined, automated money management system that requires a small amount of effort to set up and very little time each month to manage. It should be automated as much as possible and require a) a conscious decision and b) several manual steps to access any money set aside for saving and investing

These rules are the same for your children: they also need an automated saving system that will remove the temptation for them to spend more money than has been allocated for that purpose. Accordingly, the lessons you'll learn in this chapter include the importance of paying yourself first (the most important one!), delayed gratification, setting both long- and short-term goals, guidelines on how much to save, and the excellent effect time has on compound interest and saving.

Maximising Simplicity and Removing Temptation

Now, before we begin: a lot of parents put money away for their child's education or first car, or some other considerable expense, and I just want to take this moment to clarify that saving/investing for your children is done *in parallel* with the below saving system. As a rule of thumb, don't put your money into your child's account. Remember the quote, 'Give a man a fish, and you will feed him for a day. Teach a man to fish, and you will feed him for a lifetime.' Let your children watch the money they've earned grow and let them learn by doing, saving, and investing themselves.

Now, let's start.

To begin applying this rule of maximising simplicity and removing temptation to your children's finances, get them into the habit of always paying into their 'saving' container first when they receive their pocket money. Foster this mindset of paying your future self first while your children are young, and by the time they start working their first part-time job, a portion of their wage will go immediately towards their savings goals—some to increase their buffer fund, and some into an investment fund for their future self. (More on this in Chapter 7.) Immediately putting this money aside will teach your children two things: delayed gratification and goal setting.

Delayed gratification involves making a sacrifice, resisting temptation, or delaying something enjoyable now so you can have something even better in the future. A goal ladder is one visual way of describing delayed gratification to young children. The below diagram uses the example of saving up to buy a phone: if they save for a short period, they might be able to buy a second-hand iPhone or a cheaper model, but if they wait for a longer period and save all the while, they can either buy the latest phone or

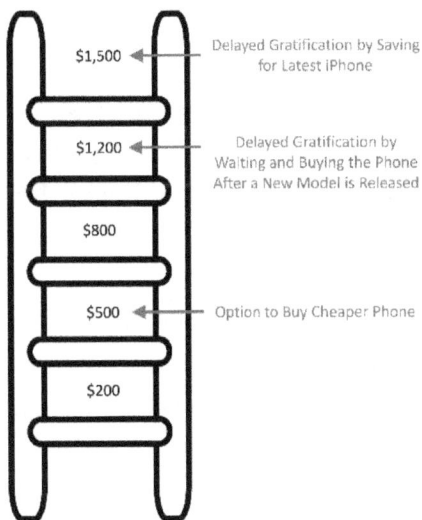

$1,500	Delayed Gratification by Saving for Latest iPhone
$1,200	Delayed Gratification by Waiting and Buying the Phone After a New Model is Released
$800	
$500	Option to Buy Cheaper Phone
$200	

a reduced-price iPhone when a new model is released.

This is a similar concept for a younger child: one week's spending money will buy a lollipop for one dollar, but if they wait for *two* weeks, they can buy a lemonade icy pole for two dollars—and if they wait for *three* weeks, they can buy a milo ice cream for two dollars and fifty cents.

A simple exercise to do with younger children to test if they have solid delayed gratification skills is to put a lolly in front of them and tell them they can eat it now or leave it there for fifteen minutes. If they do the latter, they can have two lollies once the fifteen minutes is up. It's not the lolly that is relevant, but the ability to wait. Delayed gratification is like any skill or habit: anyone can learn it with enough repetition and reinforcement.

To put this idea of delayed gratification into context, when do you spend the money in your 'saving' container?

Saving is where goal setting comes in. As Earl Nightingale said, 'People with goals succeed because they know where they're going.' The 'saving' money will help your child learn the skill of goal setting, which is critical for developing grit and getting what they want out of life. Goal setting teaches children to take responsibility for their behaviour (what they spend money

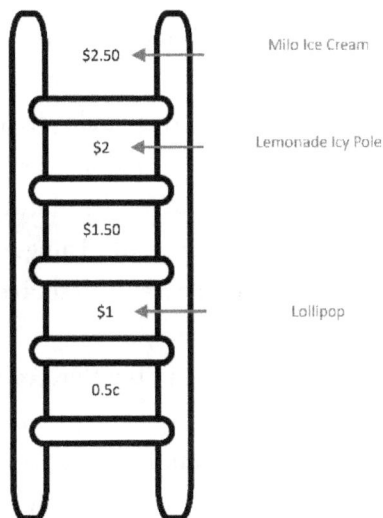

$2.50	Milo Ice Cream
$2	Lemonade Icy Pole
$1.50	
$1	Lollipop
0.5c	

on, when they spend, and why they spend) and helps form a powerful lifelong habit.

So, how do you explain what a goal is and how it differs from a wish?

A goal is something your child wants to have or do, but doesn't yet have the money, time, or permission for. These are called resources. Hence, they need to figure out what resources are required for them to have/do it in the future, and make a plan accordingly.

Notably, a goal must be something the *child* wants, and needs to be written down using the "SMART" format to be most effective. We'll go through the SMART structure in detail a bit later, but for now, you can use the following simple activity to help explain to your child what a goal is.

1. The first step is to figure out what your child wants. Figuring this out might take a few conversations over dinner or in the car just to get them thinking. The first time you ask, you might get a blank stare or a lengthy wish list of all the toys and treats they can think of, so persevere with this until you get an accurate answer!

2. When they're ready, ask your child to write down (or tell you so you can write down) all the things they want to have, be, or do.

3. Now, take another piece of paper with three columns labelled 'now', 'later', and 'resources', and ask them to put the items on their list into either 'now' or 'later'. Things that go into the 'now' column are things they could physically do now with the resources they already have (such as buy a small lollipop at the shop with the five dollars they got for their birthday last week, or jump on the trampoline in the backyard). Things that go into the 'later' column are things they don't have the resources to do yet, such as buying a new bike or an iPhone.

4. Lastly, in the third column, write down what they would need or what is holding them back from getting the items in the 'later' column. These might be more money or Mum's permission.

5. Next, explain to your child that the items in the 'now' column are *not* goals, as these could theoretically happen straight away. The

items in the 'later' column, however, could be goals if the child did (or had) all the things in the resources list (which generally will concern time and money).

6. Explain that goals have specific steps that you must take within a certain timeframe to achieve them. This makes goals different from 'wish' items written on a birthday list where no action is required— except waiting for the birthday to arrive, that is!

WISH	GOAL
Get a new Lego set.	Save five dollars a week for ten weeks to buy a fifty-dollar Lego set.
Do a cartwheel.	Practice doing cartwheels for ten minutes every afternoon for the next two months.

Again, for a goal to be practical for children, it not only has to be SMART, but, most importantly, it must be something *they* want (not that *you* want) so they don't lose motivation. The goal also needs a timeframe that is appropriate for their age so they, again, don't lose motivation. A helpful rule of thumb for younger kids is one week of saving for each year of age. So, for example, six weeks of saving would be the limit for a six-year-old. Having mini rewards at certain milestones is also very useful, especially for longer timeframes.

So, what are SMART goals?

SMART stands for:

- Specific (something they want and know when they have).
- Measurable (something they can track, such as by a number or percentage).
- Achievable (something they can achieve on their own, with little to

no assistance).

- Relevant (something that will make them smile and that they genuinely want).
- Time-bound (something that has a deadline).

Below are some steps that will help you to set practical goals for your children and track their progress with them and, in turn, help your children to stay motivated during the process.

Step 1: Let Them Choose the Goal

Choosing is essential, as your children need to have ownership over the decision they make. That doesn't mean they should pick the first thing they say. For this to be a positive experience and one they'll want to repeat again and again until it becomes a habit, we want to help them filter down all the goals and dreams they have to *one* goal that they can achieve relatively quickly.

Note that this goal needs to equate to more than one week's (and thus one payday's) worth of work. Otherwise, it's not a saving goal; it's just spending. Then again, too long of a window, and small children may struggle with understanding delayed gratification. Hence, a balance needs to be struck here.

You may find using the 'quick-win goal' circle below useful to help your kids to determine the cheap and expensive goals they have, and whether they want them a lot or a little.

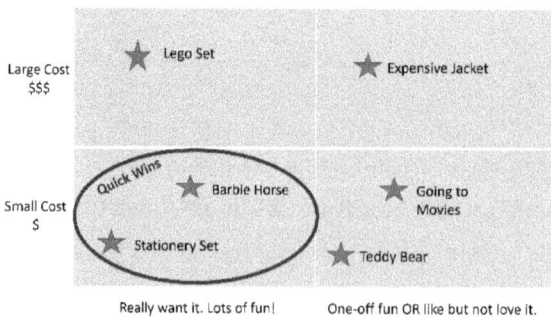

Large Cost $$$	★ Lego Set	★ Expensive Jacket
Small Cost $	Quick Wins ★ Barbie Horse	★ Going to Movies
	★ Stationery Set	★ Teddy Bear
	Really want it. Lots of fun!	One-off fun OR like but not love it.

Step 2: Discuss the Purpose of the Goal

Why do they want this? And how will this help others? Understanding this will assist with their motivation and keep them going.

For example:

- My daughter wanted to use her savings on a toy horse for her Barbies so they could have something to ride and so she could learn to plait hair by practicing on the mane.
- My other daughter wanted to learn to do cartwheels so she could be in the front section of the Christmas concert. She thought it would make the performance more enjoyable.

Step 3: Write Down the Goal

If the child is old enough, they should write this themselves; if not, parents can assist. Either way, keep this somewhere visual to remind your children of it when they add to their 'saving' container each week.

Below is an example of what we keep laminated next to our money containers. We colour the thermometer to show how close we are to the savings goal. We discuss this goal and choose a different charity every three to six months.

Step 4: Break the Goal Down into Smaller Steps

This will help children to focus on the process instead of just on the outcome. Smaller, incremental goals can help to keep them motivated. By having these in place, they are continuing to practice the skills while celebrating their successes along the way.

Name.. Date...

I am saving for... My charity is ....

I need.................by... Because...

Amount needed = $

Amount saved so far = $

Number of weeks left
to save =

Starlight
Children's Foundation

Step 5: Brainstorm Obstacles

So that your child doesn't lose the motivation needed for them to achieve their goals, it's often good to talk about what obstacles or things could go wrong while they work towards the goal and to come up with a few ideas or actions they could do to prevent or, at least, mediate these.

For example, when saving to go to the movies during the school holidays, we realised that with only four weeks to go, my daughter would not have quite enough money—so we negotiated some extra jobs she could do each week (such as washing the car) to get the extra five dollars she needed.

Multiple Goals

As your child gets older, they may wish to have more than one savings goal. You can download different goal-saving examples at www.kidsfinance.com. au/resources.

Savings Goals

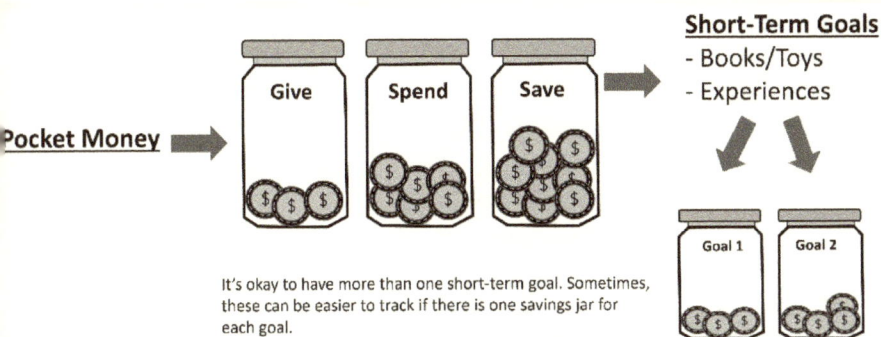

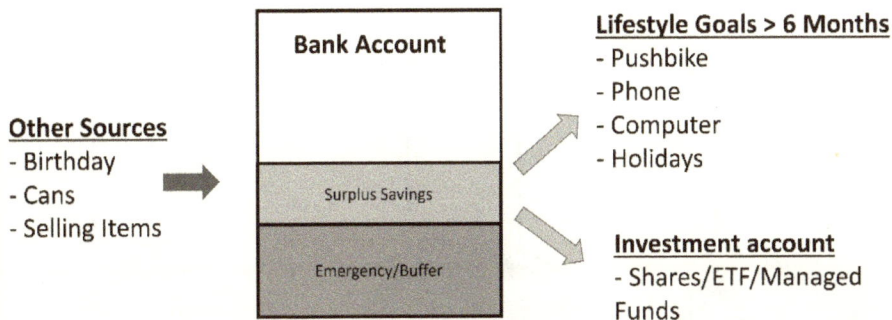

Pocket Money →

Give | Spend | Save →

Short-Term Goals
- Books/Toys
- Experiences

Goal 1 | Goal 2

It's okay to have more than one short-term goal. Sometimes, these can be easier to track if there is one savings jar for each goal.

Other Sources
- Birthday
- Cans
- Selling Items

→

Bank Account

Surplus Savings

Emergency/Buffer

Lifestyle Goals > 6 Months
- Pushbike
- Phone
- Computer
- Holidays

Investment account
- Shares/ETF/Managed Funds

Check the lifestyle goals and emergency buffer account every few months. Children will probably be around eight to ten years old before they are interested in investing.

Savings Goals: Example

Goal #1: Pedicure
How Much: $36
Source: Pocket Money
How Long: 9 Weeks
($4/Week)

Goal #2: Book Club
How Much: $16
Source: Birthday Money
How Long: N/A

Goal #3: SeaWorld
How Much: $50
Source: Pocket Money +
Birthday Money
How Long: 10 Weeks

Goal!

$35

$28

$21

$14

$7

$0

Goal!

Goal!

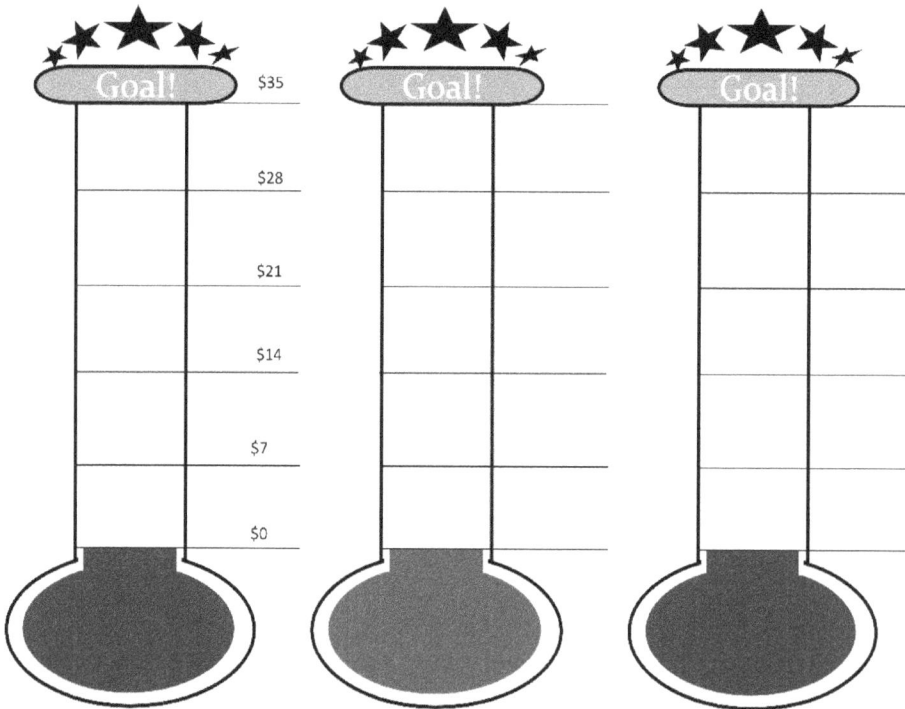

Total Pocket Money Saved: Total Birthday Money:

Bank Accounts for Children

As well as their 'saving' containers, my children also have a buffer fund, which is an online bank account used for longer-term goals. I mentioned earlier that my children also earn additional money through collecting cans or are sometimes given birthday or Christmas money from relatives, and this additional money I put directly into their bank account so they can start building up their emergency/buffer fund. Importantly, they know these funds are there, and they understand that it is important to put money away for the future, though we periodically look at these funds to show that the balance is growing in mind of the interest that is being paid from the bank.

This leads to the question of, what type of saving bank account should you open for your children?

Ideally, this should be an online, high-interest, no-fees saving account, but for simplicity while the kids are young, it might be simpler to open an additional bank account with your current bank and add their name as a 'nickname'. Just check that there are no additional fees attached to this. To reduce fees, some savings accounts may require balances to be greater at the end of the month than at the beginning, and if this is the case, set up a direct debit from your account of fifty cents per month to be transferred. I use this small amount of money to teach my young children about the concept of interest.

You can explain interest to your kids as the money the bank pays you to borrow your money. The longer you leave it in the bank, the more money the bank will give you and the more you will have. Once you explain this, your children will likely get excited at the prospect of making money without them physically doing anything.

Opening a savings account is an excellent way to introduce your kids to banking, saving, and interest. However, be aware that a bank account might seem like something of a black hole for younger children who find it quite tricky to understand—so to counterbalance this, show them the bank account (either on an app or computer) with their name every few months so they can begin to familiarise themselves with the interface. It would also be helpful to go into the bank every few months with physical cash to deposit into your accounts so they can really start to make the connection between physical money and their bank account.

Simple Interest and Compound Interest

This seems an appropriate place to do a bit of a deep dive into simple and compound interest so you can understand precisely what these two different types of interest are, explain them to your children, and, most importantly, begin reaping the benefits of compound interest!

Before we begin, though, you can explain the concept of interest to your children as follows: if there is something you have that someone else needs/wants and you don't need right now, you can lend it to them and they will pay you something to borrow it for a certain period. For example, one of my daughters had a teddy she didn't need for a day, so she lent it to her sister and in return, her sister agreed to give her two stickers. Similarly, if we have money we don't need straight away, we can put it in the bank, and the bank then pays us money (called interest) for borrowing our money. If we agree to lend it to the bank for a longer period (e.g., six months), they will pay us a higher amount. This is often referred to as a term deposit.

Another example of this might be property investing, where you own a house but don't need it straight away, so you lend it to someone else for a period of time (e.g., a twelve-month lease agreement) and the tenants pay you money (known as rent) to live in the house.

As we briefly touched on previously, simple interest is where the interest is calculated based on the principal (i.e., the original) amount only. For example, let us say we had 10 lollipops and an interest rate of twenty percent per year. With Simple interest, this equates to an extra two lollipops per year—(twenty percent of ten lollipops is 2) meaning after one year, there will be twelve lollipops, after two years, there will be fourteen lollipops, and so on.

Compound interest, on the other hand, puts the interest (or additional lollipops) to work, too. That is, it also takes into account the additional lollipops you earned when calculating your interest, rather than just the amount you started with. Therefore, during the second year of compound interest, instead of earning interest on the original ten lollipops, you'd make interest on the *twelve* lollipops, (twenty percent of twelve lollipops is 2.4 lollipops in the second year) meaning after ten years, there would be sixty-two lollipops (compared to the thirty lollipops after ten years earned using simple interest).

Compound interest vs Simple interest (20%)

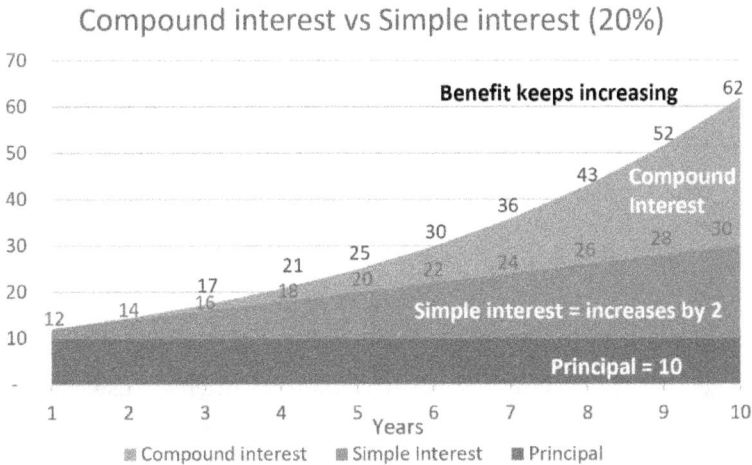

The difference may seem small, but what if this was to compound for thirty years? Using simple interest, this would give 10 lollipops + (30 yrs*2 lollipops) = 70 lollipops. Now, of course, you could theoretically eat all these additional lollipops as and when you get them—but how many lollipops do you think there would be if you *didn't* eat them straight away and instead left them there (re-invested using compound interest instead of simple interest)? In other words, what would happen if you used delayed gratification? Two hundred lollipops? Five hundred lollipops?

No: **two thousand three hundred lollipops.**

That's a lot of lollipops!

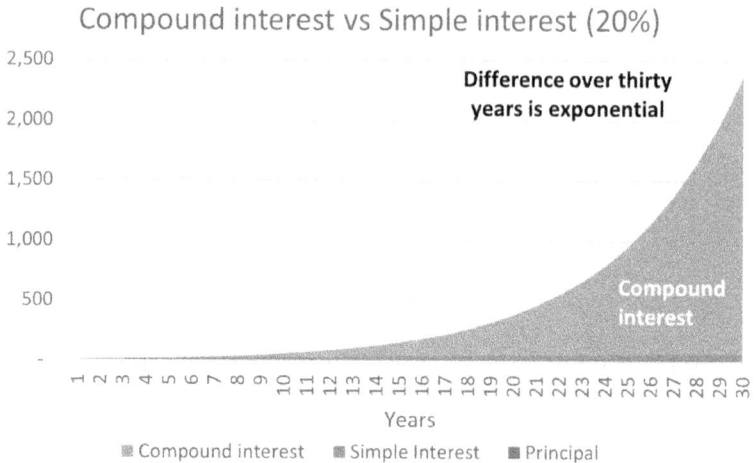

Compound interest vs Simple interest (20%)

Difference over thirty years is exponential

Compound interest

Years

▦ Compound interest   ▪ Simple Interest   ▪ Principal

Now imagine if that was money instead of lollipops!

The key lesson here is that your savings will grow faster if they are invested in an account that uses compound interest instead of simple interest. The higher the interest rate and the more frequently it is compounded (daily vs monthly), the faster the money will grow.

However, the real magic with compound interest comes with time... so we will dive into more detail later in this book about how superannuation and various share portfolios use compound interest to grow your balance, which will help you reach financial independence quicker.

We've covered a lot of ground in this chapter, so let's have a look at the following case study to really contextualise our learning. Below, you can find the saving systems we have set up for our six-year-old daughter, Emma, in alignment with everything we have discussed in this chapter.

1. Emma does three age-appropriate jobs a week and is paid six (her age) dollars per week for doing this.

2. She has a small shoebox that she keeps her three containers and wallet in. Stuck at the top of the box is her saving thermometer (a template for this can be downloaded at www.kidsfinance.com.au/resources), which clearly states the short-term goal she's saving up for and how much she needs to save in total to reach it.

3. Fifty percent of her pocket money goes into her 'saving' container. This is the first amount she puts away each week. Then, the total in the 'saving' container is counted and the coloured thermometer is adjusted accordingly.

4. One dollar goes in the 'giving' container and the rest goes into her 'spending' container (or straight into her wallet).

5. Money given to her from relatives or earned from collecting cans goes into a bank account with her name on it (just a 'nickname' in my personal bank). Birthday and Christmas money is split between buying something straight away for herself and saving.

6. I have set up an automated transfer of fifty cents month to go into her bank account to teach her about 'interest'. This also allows us to avoid fees from the bank, as the balance needs to increase each month as part of the terms and conditions of a fee-free saving account.

7. Every few months, we look at the balance of the bank account. My daughter knows this money is for when she is older.

8. Like nearly every child, she has a long-term saving goal for a phone or a puppy.

9. When she reaches about ten years old, she'll be introduced to the share market and, provided her buffer account is at the required level, she'll start investing (including re-investing dividends) to make the most of the effects of positive compound interest. (More

on that in Chapter 7.)

10. By the time she starts working her first part-time job, she'll have a low-fee superannuation fund with an eighty to one hundred percent growth allocation—which means most of her superannuation funds will be invested in the stock market. (More on that in Chapter 10.)

You need to be confident that your child knows the importance of saving and will have enough saved for a rainy day by the time they hit adulthood. These lessons, however, aren't just about having 'enough', but are also about the enjoyment and happiness of giving to and sharing with others. After all, who doesn't want to give their child the gift of happiness?

Section Activities

In line with the above, your activities for this section are as follows:

- [ ] Get a bag of M&Ms, Skittles, marbles, or pompoms. You can choose to do this either over five days or all at once by making five piles. Let your child know that there are two choices: the first is you giving them one skittle each day (so a total of five skittles) and them eating these whenever they choose. The second option is them leaving the skittles in a pile and you doubling the amount in the pile every day. Before they choose, have them watch as the pile goes from Day 1 = 1, Day 2 = 2, Day 3 = 4, Day 4 = 8, and Day 5 = 16. Alternatively, if you have a big bag, you could do this for seven or fourteen days! This will visually illustrate the power of compound interest.

- [ ] Establish a short-term savings goal with your child and create a budget and savings plan so they can get there (for example, save three dollars per week so the fifteen-dollar goal will take five weeks to achieve). Make it visual by drawing or writing what they're saving for on a whiteboard or printing a 'thermometer' image that they colour in as they get closer to their goal. They can even cut a picture of their desired item out from a catalogue and stick it to their container or chart.

- [ ] Open a no-fee bank account (preferably one paying high interest) with your current bank and add a 'nickname' for your child. Then, every few months, show your child how much the balance has grown. (Note: With the current cash interest rate so low, you may need to set up an automatic transfer of fifty cents or one dollar per month from your account to your children's account to teach this lesson.)

- [ ] Understand the effect of compound interest. Go online and put...

Section Activities (Continued)

...varying amounts, interest rates, and periods of time into a compound interest calculator. A good one that also has an alternate strategy section to compare can be found on the Australian government Moneysmart webpage at: www.moneysmart.gov.au/ budgeting/compound-interest-calculator.

Key Takeaways

- You're never too young (or old) to set up a system where you automatically put money away into savings first and then give a little bit before spending the remainder.
- Compound interest is often called 'interest on interest', as the interest earned is reinvested along with the principal amount to create a snowball effect. This means the amount grows 'on' itself, gaining momentum over time, and plays a significant role in saving and borrowing money as children learn to understand the impact. Should you incorporate this into their personal finance learnings, they'll be more encouraged to save earlier and avoid credit card debt.
- Make sure you have an emergency buffer fund set up early and that it grows as your children grow. You'll want to aim to save around one thousand to two thousand dollars for when they leave school to pay for a bond, rent, or money towards a car.

5

Giving

In a world where you can be anything, be kind.

—UNKNOWN

Do you remember the smile on your toddler's face when they asked if you wanted their half-eaten biscuit? The expectant look on their face and then the big smile when you started to eat it? This was not just the act of giving; it was the act of seeing the person *enjoying* eating the biscuit that brought your toddler their delight.

The joy of giving and sharing is one of the best feelings in the world. A good friend of mine, Mel, can remember that as soon as she got her pocket money each week as a child, she'd go down to the corner store and buy a packet of mixed lollies from the counter. She'd then bring them straight back to share with her brother and sister. This is a happy memory for her. Mel also recalls her mother once telling her that she didn't have to share them every week, as her brother and sister could buy their own—but when she tried this out and didn't share, she learned a valuable lesson: it wasn't the lollies in and of themselves that brought her the joy, but the act of sharing and eating them with her siblings.

This chapter will focus on creating opportunities for your children to continue to grow and experience the rewarding gesture of giving, making other people smile, and feeling grateful for what they currently have.

There are two main ways in which you can reinforce the act of giving: one is talking about it, and the other is modelling this physically by giving your time (by volunteering) or your possessions (by offering second-hand goods or money) to others.

Explaining to young children the importance of giving isn't difficult: they learn from an early age that it is kind to share their toys, and they see firsthand the delight in other children when they play together and the unhappiness in other children when they're not shared with. The concept of giving our money or time is no different: we give what we can to make other people smile.

My children and I often discuss these things, as well as all the different charities out there and how we don't have to give much—just a few dollars—to make a huge difference.

My daughter was very excited the first time she received a small gift from her charity, Koala Rescue QLD. She was so proud that she took it into school to show her teacher, and she then conversed with her teacher (who she admires) about the charities to which she (her teacher) donates. This simple three-minute conversation stuck with her, and she came home very excited to tell me that her teacher donates to help kids with cancer.

My point? The more you, as a parent, talk about giving, the likelier it will be that your child gives and volunteers themselves.

So, how do you introduce your children to the concept of giving away their money?

The straightforward way to start is by using the saving system discussed in the previous chapters—that is, when they receive their pocket money each week, paying their future self by putting twenty to fifty percent into their 'saving' container. The next step is to put some in their 'giving' container. We don't have rules regarding how much to put in each week, so long as something goes in. Some weeks, the girls put in fifty cents; other times, they put one dollar. Either way, the critical message is always to give *something,* no matter how little. After a while, they realise that the more money they have in the 'giving' container, the more they can help.

My children didn't understand this process straight away; they'd worked hard to earn their pocket money, and now they were supposed to give it away? However, it didn't take them long to grasp the concept, and they now enjoy deciding who to give this portion of their earnings to—and as they get older, they'll even better understand that by being generous, they're positively impacting the community and making the world a better place for everyone.

Charities

We first formally introduced our children to charities when we set up their 'giving' jar as part of the saving system we implemented. To do this, I first researched a few charities in each category that I thought would interest my children (for example, animals or sick children). One of my reasons for researching first was so I could check the minimum donation amount and their terms regarding the acceptance of one-off donations or monthly contributions. I also wanted to check if they posted information by mail instead of electronic communication, as children *love* receiving mail in the post, especially as they start to learn to read!

I then shortlisted each category, talked to our children about who they wanted to help, and read the stories about the charities on the computer as part of the decision-making process.

In the end, my four-year-old decided she wanted to help sick animals, so she donated her 'giving' money to the RSPCA—and now, each month, they send her a pamphlet with stories about all the animals they've helped recently. As you can imagine, she loves hearing about all the animals, and gets excited when her mail arrives each month.

Name: Emma

I am saving for: Bowling

I need $30 by School Holidays

Date: November

My charity is: Koala Rescue QLD

Because: There are not many left.

Goal!

Amount needed = $

Amount saved so far = $

Number of weeks left to save =

Starlight Children's Foundation

After the children have chosen their charity, they print out a picture to stick on their 'giving' container or write it on their goal board.

Note: Don't let the 'giving' container get too full, or your children will start to resent putting money in there instead of saving and spending. They need to see that this money is helping others regularly. So we can keep the concept of giving fresh, we choose a new or additional charity for them once every three to six months (usually when my daughters' 'giving' jars are getting full). This ensures that giving remains exciting and somewhat of a novelty for them.

Presents

Another option for children to spend their 'giving' money on is presents for others. This results in instant gratification for your kids (important in balance so your kids can remain motivated and empowered by their finances). Examples might be buying flowers for an elderly neighbour or small gifts for their friends. This will also allow them to be on the receiving end of sincere gratitude, which is great for them!

The annual Christmas toy drive (usually run by Anglicare or another charity) is another opportunity for children to buy a small gift for those who are less fortunate.

Charity Shops

A simple and easy way to give is to donate pre-loved toys and clothes to the local op/charity shop, such as Lifeline, Vinnies, or the Salvation Army. Every six months or so, we go through our belongings and decide which things we no longer want or need. Some of these items we sell, but most (mainly toys and clothes) we donate to a charity shop so they can be available to others who might not be as fortunate as us.

To make this experience more effective, the children should take their belongings in and hand them over themselves. I've also found it to be a good idea to call ahead to organise a suitable time to drop off at the charity, especially for the first time: explain that this will be the first time your child is giving away their toys to ensure the person collecting the items will have the time to properly acknowledge and thank your child. After all, your child may emerge very disappointed if they hand over their belongings or 'giving' money and are either ignored or brushed off without a thank-you! Further, as they start to give regularly, they might get to know the volunteers who work there, and this will make this experience even more memorable for the children.

When my children donate their clothes and toys, they sometimes take a few dollars from their 'giving' container to donate or buy something for themselves. All proceeds from the charity shop go towards helping those in need.

We also visit charity shops when we need costumes instead of going to large department stores. These are great places to find treasures, and have the added benefit of allowing you to save money by buying second-hand. Plus, the proceeds go to charity!

Santa Sacks

Christmas is a great time to introduce new traditions, such as the Santa sack tradition—and no, this isn't leaving a sack for Santa to fill with toys, but instead leaving a bag full of toys *for* Santa! Leaving presents is another way to help children learn the importance of giving back and thinking of others from a young age.

The concept is simple: your children fill their Santa sack/stocking with toys they either no longer want or wish to give to less fortunate children, and leave this for Santa on Christmas Eve. Santa then takes the toys on Christmas Eve to give to children who are less fortunate. This is also a great way to make room for more toys that Santa may bring!

Choose a method for the Santa sack tradition that suits your family. For example, you may wish to let the children choose the toys themselves, or you may wish to gently guide them. It might be helpful to select all the toys at once, or it might be more manageable to add one toy at a time leading up to Christmas.

Some ideas for using Santa sacks include:

- Giving a large Santa sack to your children when you start to decorate the house for Christmas and explaining to them that they are to fill it with things they no longer love. Santa will then share them with other boys or girls who don't have many toys.
- If you are incorporating the 'Elf on a Shelf' tradition at Christmas, you could merge the 'Santa sacks' tradition with this by asking the elf to leave a special note written from Santa explaining what to do.
- When your kids open their *actual* Santa sacks/stockings on Christmas morning, use a drawstring sack so the children can take it in turns to pull one gift out at a time so they can appreciate each one.

Once the children are older, the Santa sack tradition can shift to taking toys straight to the charity shops and donation centres.

Birthday Parties

When my eldest daughter invited her entire class to her birthday party, we were excited that so many could make it. Of course, everyone had a great time, but I underestimated how generous everyone would be! The number of presents she received was enormous.

To balance this out a little, we spaced the present opening out across a span of time by opening only one or two per day. This allowed her to play with and appreciate each gift individually.

One of my good friends also had a great idea for her son's party: she asked that the guests bring cash in a card. Half of this money would be used by the son to buy something for himself, and the other half would go to his choice of charity.

The party was a huge success: he chose a few large items from the shops that he wanted, and the kind people at YAPS (one of our local animal rescue shelters) made a big deal out of his donation when he took it in.

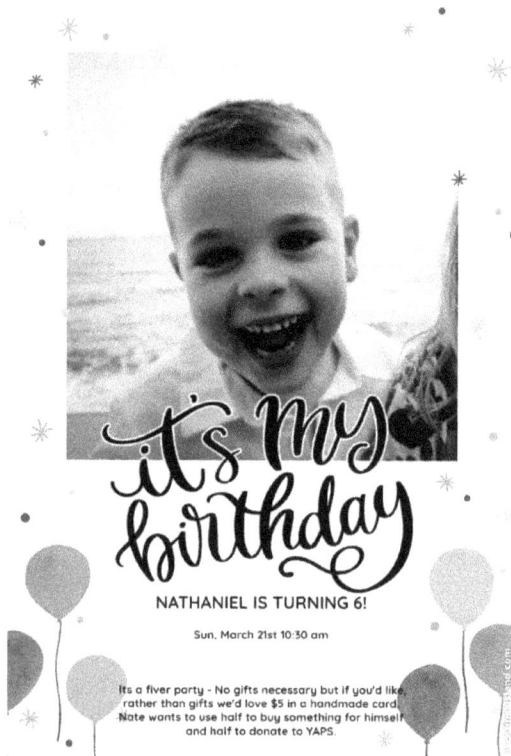

NATHANIEL IS TURNING 6!

Sun, March 21st 10:30 am

It's a fiver party - No gifts necessary but if you'd like, rather than gifts we'd love $5 in a handmade card. Nate wants to use half to buy something for himself and half to donate to YAPS.

Helping the Homeless

My parents often talked to us about how lucky we were while growing up in Australia. When they were young, they'd done extensive travel, and so they organised school exchange programs for my siblings and I to Japan and China in high school. I think this was partly for the travel experience and partly so we could appreciate the life we led in Australia. Regardless, this lesson stuck with me, and I remember sponsoring numerous overseas children as soon as I started earning money.

Having small interactions with people in need is an opportunity to teach compassion and empathy. For example, if I'm with my daughter and someone asks for money or help on the street, we look the person in the eye and say, 'Hello. We hope you have a good day. Good luck,' and hand over a bit of money. To always ignore them or cross to the other side of the street to avoid them is inadvertently teaching your children to ignore other people who are hurting.

I now also keep a small Ziploc with a few dollars and a piece of paper listing a few local charities in my handbag that we give to people who need help. There are many charitable organisations such as 'Rosies—Friends on the Street' where homeless people can get a decent meal and have a talk to someone instead of being alone, and so it's critical that you share this information with those in need whenever you can.

Remind your kids after having these conversations that we shouldn't feel guilty that we have better health or more material things than others. Instead, we should feel grateful.

Section Activities

- ☐ Talk to your child about the charities or organisations to which you currently donate your money or time and why they're important to you. (You don't have to donate much; it's the act of giving, not the amount, that's important.)
- ☐ Make a shortlist of charities for your child to give to and pick a charity together.
- ☐ Together, look through toys and clothes and find some items to donate to the local op/charity shop. Also, take their 'giving' money (if they have some) to spend at the local op/charity shop and explain that the money collected is used for food and other essential items people need.
- ☐ Keep a small Ziploc with a few dollars and a piece of paper with details of a few local charities written on it in your handbag to give to the homeless when you want to.

Key Takeaways

- • The gift of giving teaches generosity and gratitude for our experiences and the things in our lives.
- • It doesn't matter if you have more or less than others; you need to be grateful for the things you have, share them generously, and spend money consciously on the things that you enjoy.
- • 'Success isn't about how much money you make; it's about the difference you make in people's lives.' – Michelle Obama

6

Spending

Budgeting isn't about limiting how much you spend, it is about prioritising what you spend it on.

One day while shopping, my daughter saw a small toy she wanted. When I explained she hadn't brought her 'spending' money to the shop, she replied, 'I don't need money. I'll just use your card.'

Unfortunately, the concept that using a card to pay for things still leads to spending 'real' money can be tricky for children to understand. After all, when *we* grew up, we saw money changing hands every day: our parents used cash to buy food at the shops, pay for fuel, and even make phone calls. It was a tangible thing that you could see and feel—but today, money is essentially invisible. Our salaries get deposited straight into our bank accounts; we transfer money via computers; we even order and pay for food, clothes, and toys online. Hence, as we move towards a cashless society, we need to teach our children about their own 'invisible' money and how to manage it. Accordingly, this chapter will show you how to find ways to talk to your children about money and how to maximise on opportunities for them to develop their spending decision-making skills. This isn't about teaching them to save and not spend, but rather to spend on things that will make them feel joy for an extended period.

*

When we talk about money, we assume there's only one type. However, one of the essential lessons you can teach your children from a young age is that there are three main types of money exchanges.

1. Cash. Cash is the notes and coins that we can physically see and touch. I've taught most of the lessons explained in this book to my own kids through cash, as this is most easily understood by children. For this same reason, my children get paid in cash so they can physically put some into their purse or wallet and hand it over at the shops in exchange for the items they want to purchase.

2. Debit. Debit is essentially the 'invisible' money that children see us using when we tap or swipe our cards instead of giving cash. We need to remind our children that this is still our money that we're using, and we must have enough in our bank account to cover the cost of our purchase. We use debit instead of cash because it isn't always practical to carry a large amount of cash for groceries or fuel.

3. Credit. Credit is when you borrow money to pay for something. The downside of credit is that you need to pay interest (extra money) on top of the amount you borrowed to spend it. (As we've covered, parents can introduce interest at an early age.) This is important because before using credit, you need to know the interest charged and when it needs to be repaid. (More about that later in this chapter.)

So, should you encourage your child to save or spend their money?

It can be challenging to find a balance between spending and saving. However, the aim is to spend some of your money on what brings you joy now, while at the same time saving towards something that will make your future life as enjoyable as possible.

I, for one, am naturally more of a spender than a saver: as soon as I have money in my pocket, I want to spend it. Therefore, it took self-control for me to develop and stick to a saving and spending plan. For example, I wanted a back deck built on our house, and as this was a considerable expense, I agreed to wait twelve months before investing money into this project—and after the twelve months, I still wanted it and loved it, and so I made the decision to invest in it. And this proved a wise decision! It has extended our living area and improved our quality of life at home significantly. Yet I still waited to make this decision so I could be sure that it would be worth the investment.

Spenders tend to be more natural givers, but have more challenging lessons to learn than savers when their money runs out. Savers, on the other hand, find it challenging to spend money both on themselves and others, and can miss out on enjoyable experiences as a result. Even some adults who are savers find it challenging to spend money, and so continually save for the future instead of enjoying the present. You need to figure out whether your children are natural spenders or savers and direct them to wise choices accordingly.

Something to remember that should help both savers and spenders is: in a saving or spending plan, nothing is hard and fast. Rather, you need the flexibility to change your saving goals. You may start your journey thinking you should save for one thing, but another opportunity might arise that makes you feel more joy. For example, my daughter was saving for a toy stable from Kmart for her toy horse for a while, and then she changed her mind and instead opted for the experience of going on the sky rail, a cable car up the side of and across a mountain that we often see but have only ridden once.

Another example from my personal life is as follows: I was saving to upgrade our car. We'd been saving for this for some time when we realised our children wanted a pool instead. We only waited six months before getting a swimming pool (we did the research, requested the quotes, knew prices were about to rise as summer approached, and knew we could afford it without going into debt), but we felt like this was long enough, and, again, this ended up being a good decision for us. The car upgrade could wait!

Both Matter

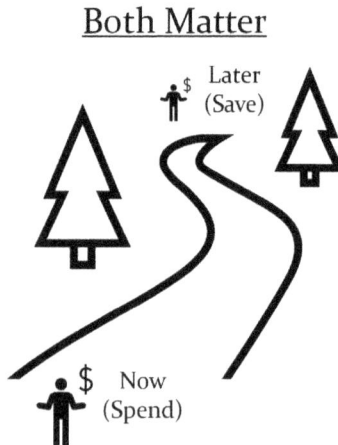

So, how can we help our children make good spending choices?

Below are some tools that can help you to assist your children in making the right spending choices.

Avoid Impulse Buying

Most children want to spend their money as soon as they have it in their pockets, so teaching them to wait before buying will help them to make wiser decisions in the future. I know for me as a kid, when I wanted something, I had to wait a certain amount of time before Mum would allow me to buy it—and in the end, this delayed gratification meant I appreciated the item so much more.

As mentioned previously, I will often take photos of toys or games that my children want and then wait for at least twenty-four hours before allowing them to make any big purchases. Beware: the trait of patience requires a lot of practice!

What you consider to be a 'big purchase' is up to you: it might be anything over fifteen dollars for a child, one hundred dollars for a teenager, or three hundred dollars for an adult. Whatever number you go with, the principle is to show children that it's okay to leave items they want in the store.

You can also use this twenty-four-hour guideline to research whether that item (or something very similar) can be bought for less at another shop or purchased as a pre-loved (second-hand) item.

For adults, I recommend extending the wait time for impulse buying to thirty days for more expensive items (such as a luxury, or a 'want' item). As mentioned previously, I even waited twelve months before committing to a significant renovation of our house! This 'waiting before spending' principle does a few things:

- It discourages impulse buying, which can be a harmful habit that's hard to break. If your children constantly see you buying things you hadn't planned on buying, it reinforces the notion that you can get everything you want when you want it on-demand.

- It takes the emotion out of the transaction. As parents, we often use shopping to improve our mood. Have you ever thought, *I'm feeling a bit down, and buying this new shirt will make me feel better*, or said to your child, 'I'll buy you an ice cream so you feel better'? I know I have! But it's vital to model for your children that there isn't always a connection between happiness and spending money. Instead, talk through the emotion and then do something fun! It allows the brain to not give in to advertising and to process whether the product will make them smile for a long time, or whether they'd prefer to spend the money on something else.

Fun Ratio

Have you ever seen a claw game? It costs two dollars per turn to try and grab a toy from a pile using a claw. Daylight robbery, if you ask me! And yet it didn't matter how many times I previously told my daughter it was a waste of money: every time we walked past the claw machine in the shopping centre, she asked to have a go. Yet when she finally used her spending money on this, it took her less than five minutes to spend over a month's worth of pocket money... to receive nothing. Try, fail. Try, fail. Try, fail. Try, fail.

It wasn't until after she'd spent all her spending money and couldn't buy any treats (like her sister could) that she started to understand the fun ratio. The fun ratio is the hours of fun per dollar that an item or activity might provide—so, for example, she could spend ten dollars on a claw machine for five minutes of enjoyment, or ten dollars on a football that she can play with every day.

Learning about the fun ratio when children are young is important, as it helps them to base their future financial decisions on the longevity of the happiness their purchase has.

Buy Second-Hand

Buying second-hand clothes and toys is becoming more and more popular. Charity shops such as Vinnies and the Salvation Army sell good-quality pre-loved belongings, and so every few months, we visit these shops to donate our unused toys and clothes and see if we can spot any bargains. These stores are also great for costumes and toys!

Facebook Marketplace and Gumtree are also great places to find items at a fraction of their retail price. For example, my girls are Lego-obsessed, so I regularly search for used Legos in my area. You can also offer a lower price when buying from markets or second-hand from someone.

Borrow or Rent

Borrowing instead of buying frees up money for purchasing items that deliver the most joy and the strongest memories. Examples of things to borrow are books and movies from the library and clothes from friends (or siblings). Several companies such as the Volte or GlamCorner rent designer clothes, shoes, and bags, too! Mobile toy libraries are becoming popular in many areas, as well.

This is particularly useful for young children at playgroups whose needs and interests change quickly.

Your children will almost definitely get the same or a similar result for a lot less money if they're aware of other options. The following are a few examples:

1. Spending money at a school café/tuckshop:
   a. Buy their lunch at school (expensive).
   b. Take a sandwich from home but buy a treat at school (cheap).
   c. Take a packed lunch from home (free).

2. Movies:
   a. See a full-priced movie at the cinema (expensive).
   b. Wait and see a half-priced movie during the holidays (moderately expensive).
   c. Rent a movie (cheap).
   d. Borrow a movie from the library (free).

3. Clothes:
   a. Buy a branded piece of clothing for full price (expensive).
   b. Wait for a sale on branded clothes or buy alternate clothes from the generic store (Kmart, Target, etc.) (cheap).
   c. Wear second-hand clothes or what you already have (cheap/free).

4. Toys and sports equipment:
   a. Buy a new toy and sports equipment (expensive).
   b. Buy used toys and sports equipment (cheap).
   c. Use what you already have (free).

The Difference Between a Need and a Want

So, what's the difference between a need and a want? Simply put, needs are expenses that can't be avoided or that make life very difficult if they're not paid. These are things like basic groceries (something to eat), rent and mortgage (somewhere to live), fuel and transport (ways to travel), education (knowledge and skills), and medical expenses.

On the other hand, a want is a non-essential expense that you *choose* to spend money on. These things should make you happy and give you the lifestyle you want, but aren't *necessary*. Examples of 'wants' are designer clothes, eating out at restaurants and cafés, and going on holiday.

Now, while basic needs such as food, water, and somewhere to live are simple examples of needs, other things are a bit more challenging to place into the 'need' or 'want' category. Clothing is an example of this.

This difference also depends on the person. For example, a professional dancer might *need* a two-hundred-dollar pair of ballet shoes. In contrast, a ten-year-old who's only just taken up the sport might only need a twenty-dollar pair.

To help you determine if something is a need or a want, ask the following three questions.

1. Is there a comparable item that costs less?
2. Can I wait a bit longer before purchasing this item?
3. Can I still do well and achieve the same result if I don't have this item?

The important thing here is for your child to understand that there's a difference between a need and a want, and that they should pause and think about whether they genuinely want to purchase this item now, later, or at all. This will teach them self-control and agency over their money. This shouldn't be about refraining from spending money at all, but recognising that they don't have to spend it at that exact moment and that they should really think about appreciate the things they do buy.

When children are babies, the parents/caregivers make all decisions for them—but as they grow, they start to enjoy making simple choices, such as the colour of their cup or what snack they have. Exposure to simple decisions (decisions that have no significant adverse consequences, that is) enhance kids' confidence in decision-making as they get older, and in the long-run, regular decision-making helps teach children responsibility and gives them the confidence to select the best option from a more significant number of alternatives.

Roleplaying grocery shopping is a great way to introduce structured spending to your kids so you can help your children to recognise the fact that money comes in limited amounts. I was very proud when my daughter saved up and bought a 'Learn About Money' set from Kmart, which came with twenty magnetic shopping items and toy money (notes and coins) so we could play shops together for this very reason.

Value For Money

Where you spend your money can have a big effect on how long your money lasts for. As an example: my six-year-old has done three jobs for the past two weeks and earned twelve dollars in total ($6*2 weeks = $12). Half of the money always goes to 'saving' (six dollars) and one dollar coin goes to her charity (Koala Rescue), leaving her with five dollars in her 'spending'. She wants to spend this money on ice cream.

Her first option is to buy the ice cream after her swimming lesson at the pool kiosk for four dollars and fifty cents. Buying straight away has the advantage of her being able to eat the ice cream immediately, but uses nearly all her money. The second option is to stop at the supermarket and buy a pack of four of the same ice creams for five dollars.

Can she wait fifteen minutes to get four times as much ice cream?

My four-year-old struggles with the wait, but kids can usually see the benefit of waiting by six years old.

(Notably, although my children can buy whatever they want with their spending money at the supermarket, I still decide when they get to eat the treats as a parent. Can you imagine the sugar high if I let her eat four drumstick ice creams in one sitting?!)

The supermarket is a great place to explain how value for money works to children: you can show that different brands of products cost different amounts, buying in bulk is generally cheaper than buying individual products, and specific products go on sale.

My children love ice cream, so a favorited lesson for them is when I set them a budget and allow them to choose a treat for the family with that budget. They look to see if any of their favourites have a half-price special on, or which of the generic brands offer the most for their budget.

Note that your kids don't always have to go for the option that is of the best monetary value; it's all about evaluation and cost-benefit. My young children generally want to spend their money on treats or toys, and while they understand that buying food from a supermarket is better value for money, they sometimes still want the instant gratification of purchasing a lollipop or ice cream when they want it—which is fine; life is meant to be enjoyed! The lesson is about making *informed decisions*. Teach your kids this, and as they get older, they'll have more confidence in their choices. Plus, as a parent, we can still watch and make sure the mistakes they make (mistakes that become essential lessons) aren't too big.

Debit and Credit Cards

Okay, so now that we've covered how we should decide *what* we should spend our money on, let's now talk about *how* we can pay for these items. Cash is a pretty intuitive concept for kids of all ages, so let's talk about the difference between a debit card and credit card and when they should be introduced.

As we've previously mentioned, children see us using our cards to pay for everyday items from a young age, so for them to develop a good relationship with personal finance, they must understand that you're still spending money by using your card. Explain that your card is linked to your account, so your bank account balance (your money) goes down a bit every time you tap your card.

If you buy something for your children with your card, ask them to get the cash from their 'spending' container as soon as you get home so they can link the card to physical money. This is very important so they can begin to make that connection from the get-go.

A credit card allows you to purchase items by *borrowing money from a bank*. In contrast, a debit card enables you to buy things using your *own money* without carrying any cash. They look similar, except debit cards have the word 'debit' written on them. They have very different benefits and risks associated with them.

Debit cards can only access the money in your *bank account*, making it convenient to make purchases without cash and limiting overspending: if there isn't enough money in the bank account, the transaction will not go through. For this reason, I recommend setting your child up with a debit card before a credit card. I believe they shouldn't get a credit card at all until they're old enough to understand both the benefits and risks of a credit card.

Of course, some people recommend avoiding credit cards altogether, but this is a personal preference. Granted, credit cards have a higher risk of overspending and getting into debt, but as a parent, I don't want my children to avoid everything that has the potential to go wrong; I'd rather they understand the benefits and risks firsthand so they can make an informed decision. To start this process, it's a good idea to introduce the idea of debt to your children from a very early age (more on this later).

Spending Plans vs Saving Goals

So, now you know how to teach your kids *what* they should spend their money on and *how* they can physically spend it. Surely that's everything you'd need to know about spending?

Nope; we need to talk about spending plans!

But what is a spending plan, and how is it different from a savings goal?

And when should you introduce children to spending plans?

A savings goal is something the child is saving up for (which usually takes several weeks or months). As we've established, it's helpful to have a poster for or a written reminder of what they're saving for and to regularly review their progress, counting how many weeks they have left before they achieve the goal.

A spending plan, on the other hand, is your child's first introduction to developing a budget. Essentially, this is a plan of how your child intends to spend their pocket money. For a young child, a spending plan can be as simple as putting fifty percent of their income towards their savings goal, followed by fifty cents towards their chosen charity, and then spending the rest of the following week's pocket money on lollipops or a small toy they saw at a shop the previous week.

As your children get older, a written plan becomes the best way to manage their money. This plan might include automating their savings into a bank account and then spending five dollars a week buying lunch at school and two dollars a week renting a movie to watch on a Saturday night.

> *Note: A spending plan is not about limiting the amount they spend, but prioritising what they spend their money on to make them happiest.*

So, how do spending plans and budgets work when special events are coming up?

I know for our family, the birthday season is a massive deal, as three out of four of us have our birthday within a month of one another! Because of this, the girls think about and plan their own party all year; the party ideas range from a mermaid-themed beach party to camping with friends to sleepovers. Their ideas also get more and more extravagant the more time passes—so a perfect exercise for them is to do a spending plan (budget) for their party—so a) their expectations don't get too outlandish and b) they can get involved in the financial side of the planning process. You can do this as follows.

1. Involve your children in planning and budgeting for a birthday party or outing. Work through all the costs such as the invitations, food, party bags, etc.

2. Let them work through the options: how many people should be invited? Which games and activities should be included?

3. Alternatively, you could set a budget and let them decide if they want games with prizes and party bags, or to go somewhere where the entertainment is provided for a cost (e.g., paying entry for their friends to be able to have the party at a waterpark).

Finding a balance between spending on the items you want today and saving for the lifestyle you want in the future can be difficult—and this can be compounded by the fear of missing out or making mistakes. Even still, as a parent, I want my children to learn from good and bad experiences, and to enable that, they need to make their *own* choices and mistakes with their *own* money (and hopefully treasure the items they buy along the way!).

My friend, Anne, remembers wanting a new pair of Converse shoes growing up. Her parents refused to buy them, so she saved her own money and still remembers the feeling of going into the shop and buying them with her own money. She's cared for and treasured these shoes ever since, and to this day, they're still the only shoes of hers that have ever stayed white!

Section Activities

We have covered a lot in this chapter, so here are some activities to complete so you can consolidate your learning and begin putting these lessons in action!

☐ Talk to your children about what they would like to spend their...

Section Activities (Continued)

...money on, and challenge/guide their selections with the fun ratio, the possibility of borrowing/renting, etc. This may not change their mind about what they want to purchase and how they want to purchase it, and that's okay, as the objective of this exercise is for your child to become aware of the options they have available to them. It's about spending intentionally, not impulsively.

☐ Talk to your kids about the difference between needs and wants. Make a list of items and ask them to sort through and mark which ones are needs and which ones are wants. Ask: what would happen if we spent all our money on wants and desires? Head on over to www.kidsfinance.com.au/resources for a pets' needs vs wants sheet as a case study. I have found this to be effective for getting younger children to really understand the difference between a need and a want.

☐ Children, in general, always find something they want, so next time they're at the shops and ask if they can buy a toy, have a quick chat about whether it's a need or a want. If it's a want, try taking a photo of it to put on their Christmas or birthday list. However, be transparent and remind them that they won't receive everything they put on their Christmas list, so to consider this carefully. Alternatively, suppose they go back to the same toy and book each time you visit the shop. In that case, it's not an impulse buy, and so you should encourage them to save up and spend their money on the item, as it will make them smile, and that is the purpose of their spending money.

☐ Next time you're at the supermarket with your children, take a few minutes to pause and include them in one of the following discussions.

Section Activities (Continued)

- o In the fruit section, show them that there are numerous types of apples, each with a different price.
- o When buying pantry staples such as flour and sugar, show them that the generic brand that tastes almost the same is less than half the price of some other products.
- o Your older kids will be able to help you find the best deal on products by looking for specials or the lowest unit price.
- ☐ To introduce debt to younger children, buy a bigger purchase that your child wants but hasn't saved up for yet. They can then 'pay it off' over the next few weeks. So they can be kept fully in the loop with this process, print out the colouring chart from www.kidsfinance.com.au/resources and mark on it how much is owed (including a bit of interest). Then, each time your child makes a payment, they can colour in a corresponding section of the chart. By the time they have coloured in all the chart (i.e., paid off their debt), they will have a better understanding of debt and the fact that it ultimately costs a bit more to get an item straight away than it does to wait until you have enough money saved.
- ☐ Alternatively (or additionally), for older children, explain an... example of good debt. This might be a home loan with a three percent interest rate when the value of the house goes up at a faster rate than they can save (i.e., greater than the interest rate you are paying on the house value).
- ☐ Before making purchases, talk about alternatives such as buying second-hand or from another store (e.g., buying food from a supermarket instead of a café or researching larger items online to find the best price).

Key Takeaways

- If you want your children to attain financial skills in life, you need to create teachable moments where they can make mistakes and learn from them.
- Most people are naturally either a saver or a spender, and as a parent, we should aim to help balance the two sides for our children and give them the tools and information they need in order to make informed decisions.
- After automating the 'saving' and 'giving' aspects of pocket money, the rest should be spent on both needs and wants. Make spending intentional.
- The money management structure you set up for both yourself and your children must save time, limit temptation and impulse buying, minimise problematic decision-making, and, most importantly, be sustainable. We will go into more detail about this in Part II.

7

Investing

Someone once told me, 'The best time for you to invest was ten years ago. The second best time is today.' This quote has stuck with me, as it's true: there never seems to be a 'perfect time' to start investing, except ASAP!

Just to recap, so far in this book, we have covered the importance of children:

1. Earning their own money so they can make and learn from their own mistakes and wins.
2. Setting up an automated savings system to create a cash buffer account.
3. Allocating time or money towards helping others.
4. Intentionally spending money on things that make them smile.

This last chapter in Part I is about investing. I've found that the quickest way to become financially independent is to invest in good-quality appreciating assets, so this chapter aims to help you explain the investment options available to your children so they can start investing early and, in turn, take the most direct route to financial independence.

There is, of course, a risk associated with everything you do with your money, from having cash assets to buying cryptocurrency and everything in between. Therefore, I'm not going to tell you exactly where to invest (even if it was legal for me to do so, which it isn't, as I'm not a financial advisor). Instead, I'm going to show you some of the tools and the structure I've set up for myself and my children.

The key is to start... and then to continue to invest at a pace that allows you to sleep at night! Below uses the tree analogy from previous chapters.

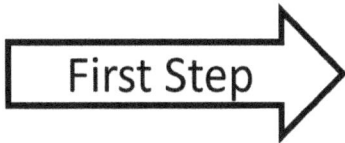

First Step — Direct at least 10% of money toward savings/investing.

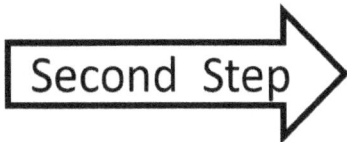

Second Step — Invest in quality income-producing assets.

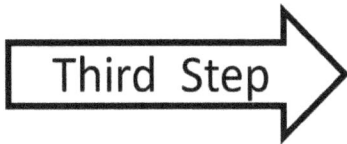

Third Step — Be patient. Reinvest dividends or make additional monthly contributions.

Explaining Investing to Your Children

The first step of investing is putting money in your bank account. Then, you can invest in the share market!

You can explain this type of investing to your children by saying that if they have money that they don't need straight away, they could put it in a bank account. This is essentially 'lending' money to the bank, and in return, the bank pays them interest. The longer you leave the money in the bank, the more interest you will receive. The benefit of lending to a bank is that you can access that money (or ask for it back) whenever you want, and it will be there.

After they have enough in their bank 'in case of emergencies', they can proceed to the next stage. There are businesses that could use your child's money to expand or build more products or services... so if your child gives some of their money to the business, the business will give them a return as a thank-you. In essence, share market investing is giving money to a business so you can share in its profits.

To illustrate this, next time you go to the supermarket with your children, stop by the milk fridge and watch how many people buy milk. Then, explain to your children that instead of putting the money they (your kids) don't need into the bank straight away, they could give it to the supermarket to buy milk from the farmers. The supermarket then sells the milk for a profit—say fifty cents more than they paid for it—and because your child gave the supermarket some money to buy the extra milk, the supermarket then agrees to pay your child five cents for each bottle of milk they sell. Count how many people stop to buy milk in the next five or ten minutes and calculate how much money your child would be paid because of this formula—and the concept of stock market investing should start to click into place!

After this, talk with your children about other businesses out there that people want the goods and services of. For example, Disney makes TV shows they want to watch, Apple makes iPads, and Toyota makes cars. It's exciting for you and your child to think about where they could start to invest their own money!

Deciding Which Income-Producing Asset to Invest in First

So, should your kids start to look to invest in the stock market immediately?

No: the income-producing asset your children should look to accumulate first is, simply, cash. Before expanding into anything else, you should ensure your child's buffer fund is at the desired level. This is essential because everyone needs to have access to some cash they can withdraw at any time, with no downside risk. As children get older, life happens, and they may lose their job, need a medical procedure, or see a great business opportunity that they want to invest in—and having this fund means they can deal with these things without facing major external consequences. For example, when the COVID-19 pandemic occurred, the stock market crashed and many people lost their jobs—and so not only did they need to access their savings to pay for their basic needs, such as groceries and rent, but those who only had savings invested in shares had no choice but to accept a significant loss in the value of their shares, as they were forced to sell them when the price was low. On the other hand, the people with large cash assets could live off the cash they'd saved in their buffer fund. Some were even able to take advantage of the situation and invest in the stock market while the prices were low!

When (and only when!) a comfortable amount of cash has been saved up, your children should start acquiring other incoming-producing assets. Part II of this book will go into more detail about the different types of portfolios to consider, as well as the different investment options.

When it comes to investing for my children's future, the strategy I have implemented is to have separate portfolios. These are broken down below.

Parent's Portfolio

This first portfolio is in my name, and is (and always will be) *my* money. This is money invested with a long-term view (greater than ten years). This portfolio aims to ensure I can help my children with their life goals when they turn eighteen. This won't be a lump sum handout to them; by following the savings strategy set out in this book, I'm confident my children will understand and have implemented sound money management strategies themselves by that point, and therefore won't need a lump sum from me! Instead, this money will put us in a position where, if we choose to, we can match their savings, whether they choose to end up putting that money towards a house deposit or university fees, as a reward or 'step-up'.

The following are a few guidelines I have used to set up our fund:

1. Set this first portfolio up as soon as possible to maximise on the benefit of time. We personally set this portfolio up when our children were babies. I chose a diversified portfolio with many asset classes such as cash, bonds, Australian shares, international shares, property, small companies, and global resources.

2. Reinvest all dividends back into the portfolio. We also make regular instalments into the portfolio, which maximises on the benefit of compound interest.

3. Review the portfolio annually to ensure it remains balanced.

4. Talk to your children about your portfolio and why you chose the asset classes, but don't tell them its true purpose (i.e., to help them) until they're eighteen.

5. Set up this portfolio on a different platform to your spending accounts to remove the temptation to sell the shares and spend this money. In my case, it takes several manual steps for us to gain access to these funds, but the monthly contribution to the fund is automated.

Don't let the fear of investing hold you back. Part II of the book goes through strategies for overcoming the fear of making a mistake or missing out, as this is a fear that can be worked through. I'll admit that it is daunting to make the decision to start, and it is hard work, and does take a while to accumulate that first one hundred thousand dollars, but you don't need to do it alone.

The example below is based on theoretically investing in the Australian Stock market.

Based on the long-term return of the Australian market of nine percent, according to www.fidelity.com.au, it would take you fourteen years to reach one hundred thousand dollars by saving and investing three hundred and fifty dollars a month, but only another six years to reach two hundred dollars, and only another four years to reach three hundred thousand dollars. This is because at the start, you are the one doing all the work, and how much you contribute will be the biggest driver of the results—but there is a tipping point at which your investments and the magic of compound interest take over. This is at about year fifteen in this example, and at this time, the investment growth is higher than the contributions, and continues to grow.

Basically, starting soon and giving regular consistent contributions is the key to building wealth. How often you contribute (daily, weekly, or monthly) is a personal preference, but once you start investing regularly, you will see your investment grow, and this will build your knowledge and confidence exponentially.

Part II of this book will look at some options, such as apps and online broking accounts, for how to start investing. You don't need a lot of money; you can invest in micro funds with a few dollars or ETFs from a few hundred dollars with Vanguard (www.vanguard.com.au/personal) or other investment organisations.

Although I have most of this portfolio invested in the stock market, you may decide that you would prefer to keep more cash (to match their savings for their first car) or to buy a property with the intent of helping them have somewhere to live while they attend university. It's completely up to you!

The purpose of this portfolio is for you to be able to help your children with the next chapter of their life without compromising your lifestyle.

Beginner's Portfolio

This portfolio is for your child. While they can't do the actual trading themselves until they're eighteen, it's never too early to get children interested in money matters!

There are several ways for parents or grandparents to invest on behalf of children as soon as they're interested—preferably by the time they turn ten to twelve years old. One of the most popular ways to purchase shares for a child is to act as the trustee, with the child as the beneficiary. That way, the shares can be transferred to your child when they turn eighteen without capital gains tax being payable.

Bear in mind the following guidelines with this:

1. Make the portfolio easily visible to your children so they can experience and learn how it grows and compounds over time.

2. Involve your children in the decision of where to invest. Likely, they will want to invest in shares of a company they're familiar with, such as Disney or Apple.

3. I recommend that children also later invest in diversified managed funds, indices, and ETFs (such as ASX 200 and Dow Jones) so they can experience the full effect of the highs and lows of the stock market.

4. Give the portfolio a mid-term view (five to ten years). The purpose of the portfolio is to give your children an experience and (hopefully!) spark an interest in investing. They may wish to sell these when they turn eighteen.

5. Beware of the effect of dividends. Tax will be payable by the person whose Tax File Number (TFN) is quoted when shares are purchased. (We'll go into this more in detail in the second part of this book.)

Again, the things to ensure you have in place before you start to invest are a) a minimum buffer account in case of emergencies and b) no debt.

It can be challenging to start, and there is a lot of information out there, but trust me, once you have the momentum going, it's rewarding knowing your wealth is increasing, your goals are getting closer, and your children are learning!

A good friend of mine, Ruby, recently decided she was ready to start investing. She'd saved a small amount and had managed to refinance her home loan to a lower interest rate. Therefore, she had a few extra dollars per month to invest. She researched online savings accounts, shares, managed funds, ETFs, and even cryptocurrencies, and found the amount of information available overwhelming and very daunting. Hence, Ruby decided to start small and invest in a well-known company. She overcame the fear of doing it alone by talking through the purchase with a friend and purchasing the shares together on the same day. This alleviated some of her fear of missing out or making a mistake. After becoming comfortable with the process and knowing that she could still save some money for her lifestyle items, such as private school fees for her boys, and some for future investments, Ruby is more comfortable knowing her money is working for her, and she is gradually getting ahead. Ruby wishes she'd known more about money and personal finance when she was growing up, and so she is now teaching her children so they can get ahead and start saving and investing early.

Our lesson here? Don't let the fear of making a mistake or waiting for the right time stop you from starting. Every year you wait just means your goals are one year further away from being achieved!

Part II of the book will show you how you can start with only a small amount of money.

Section Activities

Before they start their investment journey, the following exercise will help give your children a better understanding of how the stock markets move.

- ☐ Ask your child to pick one or two companies they wish to buy shares from (e.g., Coles or Disney). The share price on the day might be worth fifteen dollars. Whatever the figure, have them give you this money. They can then start to track the share price over time. This can be done by looking in the newspaper or on Google and recording the share price each day in a spreadsheet or on a chart so that your child can get an understanding of the fact that the price of the company they choose will go up or down on a daily basis. It might go up to eighteen dollars or down to twelve dollars, and so on and so forth.

- ☐ You can also introduce dividends to explain how the company shares its profits with people who have invested in them. (Although dividends are only paid a few times a year, you could add this in as a given percentage per week.)

- ☐ The last step is then to allow your child to make the decision of when to sell the share. There might be a spike in the price when a new Disney movie is released, and you can then give your child the theoretical money they would have earned back. Although it won't be a lot by our standards, it will be to a ten-year-old, and will hopefully spark their interest in investing. If you haven't already done so, set up different saving accounts for different purposes. For example:
    - o An emergency buffer account (an online account with no fees and preferably paying high interest).
    - o A short-term savings account for lifestyle items. For children...

Section Activities (Continued)

...this will act as their 'saving' container.

- An investing account where money is kept before shares are purchased, again with no fees and preferably high interest. To minimise brokerage fees, it can be beneficial to save a principal amount before investing.

- Start researching which types of investment you'd like to invest in and have a goal of how much you would like the balance of your parent portfolio to be worth. As an example, I want to have an investment of one hundred thousand dollars for when my five-year-old child turns eighteen.

  - To help you figure this out, there is a good compound interest calculator at www.moneysmart.gov.au/budgeting/compound-interest-calculator, where you can input the initial amount, regular contributions, and compound interest rate to give you an idea of how long your goal will realistically take. Remember that in reality, this is not a linear graph: the growth rate will be higher in some years and might even be negative in other years.

Key Takeaways

- *Always* pay yourself first. That is the greatest secret to saving and investing! As soon as you are paid, transfer between ten and fifty percent of your money directly to a savings and an investing account.

- The most direct way to reach financial independence is to invest in high-quality income-producing assets.

- Investing takes patience and is not a get-rich-quick scheme. You need to take a medium- to long-term view and make sure you have adequate funds saved in your buffer account before investing, so you only need to sell assets when suits you not in an emergency. Investing is not a race, but a slow and continuous uphill climb.

- You don't have to know exactly what to invest in yet; we will go through the *how* behind investing in Part II. For now, it's important to acknowledge the *why* behind putting money away to invest in quality assets that will grow your wealth and get you financially ahead.

- Children have an abundance of time on their hands. Therefore, the sooner they begin to invest, the greater an effect compound interest will have on their share portfolio (especially if all dividends are reinvested).

PART II

KIDS, IT'S *NOW* ABOUT THE MONEY

8

Pay Yourself First

Do not save what is left after spending, but spend what is left after saving.
—WARREN BUFFETT

The second part of this book contains more detail on several of the topics covered in Part I, but is aimed at parents who want to build on the foundational steps discussed there for either themselves or their teenage children who are starting their first part-time jobs (or the teenagers themselves!).

In other words, instead of focusing on teaching values, it is now time to focus on building wealth for the future by taking small, intentional steps. Remember, the magic of compound interest is time! Small, regular saving now will lead to the largest returns in the future.

Before getting into detail about our next teachings, it is worthwhile at this point to recap why being financially independent is a worthwhile goal. Financial independence means having multiple sources of income that provide you with enough income to live the lifestyle you desire for the length of time you desire *without* you having to do any work you don't want to do.

As mentioned previously, having multiple sources of income adds security in case something happens to your main source of income, but it also means that you don't necessarily *need* a wage earned from working for someone else. That doesn't mean you have to retire; it just means you have the *choice* of whether you work for someone else or pursue a hobby or different business idea.

One path to financial independence is:

1. Always pay yourself first. Save first and then live on what's left.
2. Avoid bad debt.
3. Invest most of your savings into quality appreciating assets that will put money in your pocket.
4. Keep reinvesting any passive income (additional income you are earning from investments) while earning a wage to supercharge the investments and increase the equity (the difference between what the asset is worth and how much you owe the bank).
5. Over time, the passive income from investments (quality appreciating assets) replaces a wage so you can choose how you spend your time.

Before going any further, I want to point out that there are a lot of different definitions of 'passive income'. Most assume that passive income is earned in a manner that requires very little or no effort, but if my experience is anything to go off, all income sources require some level of effort to acquire and maintain. To elaborate on this, Chapter 10 will go through some of the benefits and risks of the different types of income, as well as the ongoing attention required to receive passive income from various asset classes. The following chapters will also provide examples and outline the framework for the three important rules of creating wealth that you should aim to master and have become automatic habits so you can attain financial independence. These are:

1. Saving (paying yourself first).
2. Avoiding bad debt.
3. Buying quality assets.

So, without further ado, let's get into Part II!

Your child starting their first part-time job is a very exciting moment: they will have more independence, start making more decisions, and have financial control over a larger sum of money. They might be tempted to spend everything they make and enjoy every minute, but, having gone through Part I of this book, you'll know that understanding personal finance means knowing how much income you are receiving and then intentionally and consciously deciding where each dollar should go. This might mean spending everything they make for the first two months, or immediately kickstarting their savings towards their car.

Either way, this chapter will teach you why you about should pay yourself first (i.e., directing money to your savings account as soon as you are paid), set an ambitious saving target, and, when your buffer account is at the desired limit, why you should direct some savings toward building wealth for your future.

So, to get us started: we have previously discussed the model of 'Earn -> Save-> Give-> Spend'. However, as your children start to consider their first job, there are two further aspects they must be aware of.

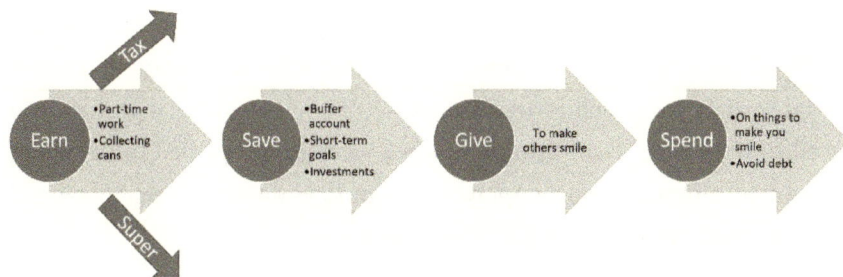

Income Tax

The first is income tax. Income tax is taken out of employees' pay by the employer before they are given their wages. The amount of tax you'll pay will depend on how much you earn and the rates set by the government. There are advanced strategies that are available that will minimise the amount you pay in taxes, but when it comes to explaining income tax to your children, the main thing they need to know is that it is compulsory to pay income tax directly from their wages. The government uses this to maintain the standard of living in your area, such as roads and medical care. More information on the rates of tax in Australia can be found at www.ato.gov.au/rates/individual-income-tax-rates.

Superannuation

The second is superannuation/your pension (or your 401K if you are in the U.S.). Superannuation is the money you set aside during your life to provide you with income when you retire. It is made up of contributions from your employer, your own personal contributions, and sometimes additional government contributions.

Generally, your employer will pay a super guarantee (in 2022, this was 10.5% of your pay) into your super account that will use compound interest to grow until you reach retirement. Note: If you are under eighteen, you need to work more than thirty hours per week to be entitled to the super guarantee, although some employers do opt to pay a smaller percentage of superannuation to younger part-time employees.

For this reason, I recommend that parents open a superannuation account for their children no later than when their children start working their first paid part-time job.

Employers will often provide application forms to their default superfund once a new employee starts their role, or you can choose to research the superfund you would like to be a part of and make your own application to join this superfund and then give details of this to employer. To do this, you'll first need to apply for a Tax File Number (TFN) for your child through the Australian Taxation Office. TFNs are free for Australian residents, and can be applied for any time from birth: simply complete the forms online, print a summary with your reference number, book an appointment at a participating Australia Post outlet within thirty days of completing the form, and bring original proof of identity documents to the meeting. For more details on this, head on over to your government's website.

Superannuation accounts are relatively easy to open, and have different investment options, which we will go through in Chapter 10.

> *The important thing is to have a superannuation fund chosen and set up before your children start working so they can allocate the fund that best suits their needs instead of using the employer's random default fund.*

After the employer has taken out income tax and any voluntary superannuation contributions, the rest of their wage should be split between saving and spending, as detailed in Part I of this book.

Bank Accounts for Older Children

While your children are little, they only need one bank account (a long-term savings/buffer account). However, as they get older, only having one will become problematic: with only one account, it will be easy to mix up (and end up spending more than intended of their) spending and saving money, and it will also be hard to determine whether they are getting ahead or not.

You may choose to start with just two bank accounts: one a savings account, the other a transactional account for spending.

If you have implemented the teachings in Part I of this book (which you should have!), you will already have a no-fee, high-interest earning savings account set up as a buffer fund. If not, this is your first step. It is best to bank savings with a different institution to your spending money so that they're out of sight and out of mind, although some banks have the ability to 'hide' an account from the dashboard so you're not tempted to spend your savings (which would have the same effect as having two different accounts). Regardless, make sure you don't have any credit cards, PayPal accounts, or any other spending connections linked to the savings account.

The second account is your transactional account for spending. This is where your salary will most likely be deposited and is what your debit/credit card will be linked to.

An important lesson (and one I keep reinforcing) and a running theme of everything I'm saying here is for you to *pay yourself first*. By this, I mean you need to automatically separate your savings from the rest of your pay check. Ideally, your employer will be happy to split your wages into two different bank accounts; if not, set up a direct debit to transfer to the savings the day after the wages go into the transaction account. The best money management is one that is streamlined and automated as much as possible.

Deciding How Much to Save

Here, I would like to introduce you to the 50/30/20 rule. The 50/30/20 rule (which was popularized by U.S. Sen. Elizabeth Warren) says that a healthy way of distributing a pay check is as follows: fifty percent to essentials (bills, food, rent), thirty percent to non-essential lifestyle items (gym memberships, clothes, mobile phones), and twenty percent to savings/investing. With that said, the more you save, the less you spend on items you might not necessarily need and the more choices you will have in life.

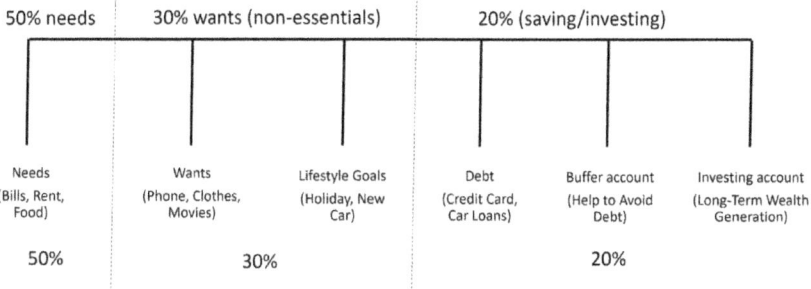

50% needs	30% wants (non-essentials)		20% (saving/investing)		
Needs (Bills, Rent, Food)	Wants (Phone, Clothes, Movies)	Lifestyle Goals (Holiday, New Car)	Debt (Credit Card, Car Loans)	Buffer account (Help to Avoid Debt)	Investing account (Long-Term Wealth Generation)
50%	30%			20%	

Something to note is that children have minimal 'needs' that they have to spend their money on, especially while they're living at home. Therefore, teenagers should set a challenging but not impossible target to save between twenty and fifty percent of their wage, as a good rule of thumb.

I recommend directing all savings into the buffer account until it has reached the desired limit before then also splitting between the other two savings accounts (short-term savings goals and investment savings).

With this in mind, to summarise the learnings of this chapter so far, your child might have the following accounts:

1. A buffer account (cash that is there exclusively to get you through financially tough times without you needing to borrow from someone else or run up a huge credit card debt).
2. An account for short-term savings goals (cars and holidays).
3. An account for investing in quality assets for future wealth.

Later, you may also wish to further split your spending account into two accounts. For example, one transactional account can be used for non-negotiable items (needs), such as rent and bills, and the other transactional account can be used for discretionary lifestyle items (wants), such as movies and eating out. Therefore, it may start with just two accounts where your child's pay is split fifty percent into each account, and over time (usually by the time children leave home), these two accounts may be further split into the following five bank accounts.

1. An emergency buffer account. Gradually increase this over time until you're at the desired limit. Note: For homeowners, some banks offer multiple offset accounts that can be used as a buffer account to reduce the amount of interest to be paid on the home loans.

2. A short-term saving account, for lifestyle/fun items, such as a new phone or car.

3. An investment account with a different institution, where at least ten percent of your salary goes on home loans/investing/debt repayments.

4. An everyday account that a salary is deposited into. After the direct debits are taken out, this will essentially be where your day-to-day expenses are purchased from.

5. A bills account to fund non-negotiable needs (as opposed to wants).

Below is a different take on the 50/30/20 rule for teenagers living at home:

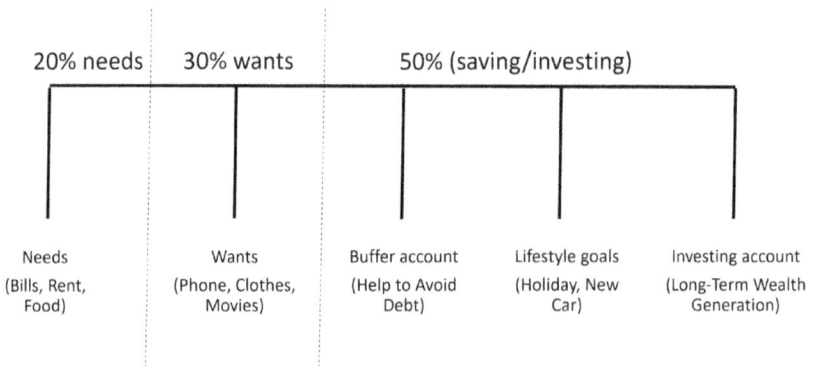

20% needs	30% wants	50% (saving/investing)		
Needs (Bills, Rent, Food)	Wants (Phone, Clothes, Movies)	Buffer account (Help to Avoid Debt)	Lifestyle goals (Holiday, New Car)	Investing account (Long-Term Wealth Generation)

Section Activities

If you are a teenager reading this (or if you are a parent reading on the behalf of your teenager), your activities for you (the teenager) to complete are:

- ☐ If you haven't done so already, open a no-fee savings bank account—preferably one that pays high interest, has no spending connections, and is invisible. If it is out of sight and out of mind, it is less likely to be spent.
- ☐ Set your ambitious savings target. Start high at fifty percent of your wage and decrease only if you need to. Even if you are stretched and just scrapping by, still put a token amount (such as a few dollars) away, and as your income increases, increase the amount going to savings.
- ☐ Automate your savings. Set up a direct debit to transfer the day after your wages go in, and whenever possible, don't rely on human actions: set your banking structure up to do the work for you.
- ☐ If your buffer account is at a level you are comfortable with, open up two other fee-free, high-interest savings accounts: one for the lifestyle items you are saving up for; one for future income-producing investments. Many banks have savings functions that allow you to set goals and will give higher interest rates if contributions are made without withdrawals.

Key Takeaways

- Pay yourself first. Automate the transfer of savings from your transactional account to your savings account.
- Increase your buffer fund over time. Without access to cash when something goes wrong, you will either need to make serious lifestyle sacrifices or go into debt.
- Without savings, you won't be able to buy assets that will eventually produce the passive income needed for you to achieve financial independence.

Pay Yourself First

Disposable Income	−	Saving + Investing	=	Spending Money

9

Avoid Debt

It's not your salary that makes you rich, it's your spending habits.
—CHARLES A. JAFFE

The habits we develop while young will help us prepare for the future, yet the world we (as in, us parents) grew up in is very different from the one our children are growing up in today. For instance, social media now exists and has a massive influence on our children, so we need them to be aware of the potential financial pitfalls that are now relevant to them so they are better prepared for the future.

Now, social media allows us to observe the belongings other people have worldwide. However, what our children see on social media isn't always accurate, nor is it necessarily a reflection of how wealthy someone is. As Will Smith said, 'Too many people spend money they haven't earned, to buy things they don't want, to impress people they don't like.'

We want our children to know the difference between being rich (having a lot of material possessions) and being wealthy. Wealthy people have the most precious asset: time. They generally have a large net worth, but they have created this for themselves by purchasing income-producing assets that ultimately buy them *time*.

Rich vs Wealthy

A story to use to help explain rich vs wealthy to children (again using trees as an analogue for investments) is as follows.

Rich people have lots of money, spend a lot of money, and show off how much money they have with material possessions, whereas wealthy people generally spend less than they earn, want to build long-term wealth, and don't need the flashiest things. They have the time to do the things they want and spend time with the people they want to.

To demonstrate, let's consider Rich Rebecca and Wealthy Wendy.

Rich Rebecca

Rich Rebecca earns a lot of money. She uses this money to make her house more and more extravagant. She buys lots of 'things' to impress people, such as cars, boats, and new clothes. Rebecca loves the fact that everyone comments on her fancy house and flash cars. Unfortunately, however, she needs to work a great deal of the time in order to afford all these things, so she doesn't fully enjoy them. Also, what everyone can't see is that out the back, there is a great big bush (i.e., her mortgage—money that she borrowed from the bank to buy the house and then add some extensions). This bush is growing larger and larger the longer she leaves it (i.e., the longer she doesn't pay any money back for). If it doesn't get pruned soon, it will be larger than the house!

Wealthy Wendy doesn't earn as much as Rich Rebecca, but she has a nice house with a pretty garden. Instead of buying cars and boats, she uses what she earns to continually prune the bush out the back (i.e., pay back the money she borrowed) so she can fully appreciate her house and use the backyard to plant more trees. Over time, these different types of trees will produce income, so she will have more time with her family and friends and she will need to spend less time at work.

Wealthy Wendy

(Pictures courtesy of Freepik)

Social media also makes impulse buying very easy: no need to wait to go to the shops or the bank to get money out! Now, we can click a button on an app or make a purchase with a credit card just by checking out of a website.

Another layer to this is the targeted advertising that comes from previous searches, making it even more tempting to spend money.

On that note, another thing to be aware of is the online scammers who use clever ways such as quizzes to gain personal information, such as a pet's name or mother's maiden name, to access accounts. Your children need to be aware that these scammers exist and to protect their personal information accordingly.

This leads us to the lesson of living within your means and avoiding bad debt. We will also cover the benefits and risks of credit cards and 'Buy Now, Pay Later' schemes, as well as setting up basic spending plans so you can direct your money to where it needs to go instead of wondering where it went every month.

To recap, I consider 'bad debt' to be any money borrowed to purchase an item that is not a quality income-producing asset. Examples include credit card debt, car and personal loans, interest-free loans to buy furniture, or even borrowing money from your sister to buy lunch. A key thing to remember here is that 'rich' people often use debt to create the *appearance* of wealth, when genuinely wealthy people avoid bad debt like the plague.

Credit Cards

We discussed credit cards briefly in Part I, and as we learned then, there are advantages and disadvantages associated with credit cards. Of course, the main disadvantage of credit cards is the risk of overspending and going into debt.

Always remember that credit cards are only beneficial if used correctly. I use a credit card instead of a debit card in my daily life (although I never say the word 'credit' when talking to my young children), but I have my bank automated so that the balance is paid off each month, so I'm not using my credit card in an unsustainable or risky way.

The reasons I use a credit card are:

- Most credit card companies offer an interest-free period, which means you can use the bank's money instead of your own without being charged any extra if you agree to pay it back before the required period. In this way, not paying for items straight away means that my money is earning me interest until the credit card payment is due.

- Credit card insurance sometimes covers the items purchased on the credit card.

- The banks generally respond quicker to fraud when a credit card has been used, as essentially, it's still their money.

- You can easily track your expenses by downloading your credit card's transaction history or reading its monthly statement. This assists with budgeting.

- It helps establish a good credit score (which indicates how likely you are to pay back the money you owe to a credit provider), which becomes invaluable when you apply for a large loan, such as a mortgage.

- Some credit cards have reward points or cashback when you make purchases using them. When this is the case, it makes sense to use a credit card instead of cash, provided you have the money in your normal bank account ready to pay off the credit card before the interest-free period ends.

A good credit score rating is only possible to achieve if your credit card is appropriately managed. Your credit score will be determined by whether you pay borrowed money back to the lender in the required timeframe. Because of this, there's a significant risk of overspending and getting into bad debt with credit cards.

The following example shows the negative consequences of misusing credit cards.

Let's imagine we make a five-thousand-dollar purchase on a credit card charging twenty percent interest. The minimum repayment is usually calculated as a percentage of the closing balance or a minimum dollar amount, whichever is higher. For this example, let's assume two percent of the balance. (This will be on your credit card statement.) If you only make the minimum repayments each month (starting at around one hundred and two dollars per month, in this case), you'll end up paying over *six thousand dollars in interest* and take more than *nine years* to pay off the amount you owe.

Talk about a lot of money! Over *eleven thousand dollars*!

However, if you pay back two hundred and fifty dollars per month, the interest paid would only be one thousand one hundred and fifty dollars, and would take just over two years (a total six thousand one hundred and fifty dollars)—or, if you can afford to pay back one thousand dollars a month, it will still cost five thousand two hundred and seventy dollars over six months.

> *Using credit will always cost you more money unless paid back within interest-free time.*

Another aspect of credit cards to be aware of is cash advances. A cash advance is when you request to withdraw cash from your credit card via an ATM or bank. This is relatively easy to do, but can be very costly: there's no interest-free period for cash advances, and the credit provider charges a higher interest rate from Day One. Further, when you make a repayment on your credit card, it goes toward your minimum repayment amount first. So, in the example above, if you withdraw one hundred dollars and repay this in full a few days later, that repayment goes toward the minimum amount (one hundred and two dollars). However, you're still being charged higher daily interest on the one hundred dollars you withdrew. So, to stop the higher interest rate, you need to repay two hundred and five dollars in that month.

'Buy Now, Pay Later' Schemes

Now to address the beast that is 'Buy Now, Pay Later' schemes.

You could buy a pair of shoes for one hundred dollars upfront, or you could purchase them using 'Buy Now, Pay Later' and pay four instalments of twenty-five dollars over a few months. There's no interest involved, it's quick and easy to sign up, and you can take your purchase home that day.

Sounds good, right? Dreamy, even?

Most people think that the 'Buy Now, Pay Later' companies make their money through late fees and interest, but in fact, the stores pay them a percentage of the purchase to offer this service. It's been cleverly designed to be convenient, allowing the customer to make no upfront payments for the product in question—but there are three distinct downsides to using the service that our children need to be aware of before they start wanting to use the service:

1. It is still debt. You are still borrowing and going into debt to get the things you want instead of saving. Avoiding bad debt is critical to being financially independent, so really, 'Buy Now, Pay Later' schemes conflict with the kind of lifestyle and mindset we're trying to create here.

2. It encourages impulse buying. This is something we have been teaching our children *not* to do in the previous chapters.

3. It encourages using debt to live above our means. Although this might only seem like a small amount now, it could be the start of a debt cycle where you constantly pay off debt instead of focusing your efforts on saving for the future.

Spending Plans

We have already discussed spending plans in Part I, but this becomes even more necessary when teens start working their first part-time job and have a little more freedom. At that point, it's essential we encourage our children to keep track of their money in accordance with their needs and wants. Note that this system doesn't have to be complicated or restrictive; all personal finance means is knowing how much money you make, how much you spend, and what you spend it on. It's about intentionally choosing what to do with each dollar.

To go about this, it can be a beneficial exercise for older children to track their spending for a week or two, record how much they spend each day, and then categorise these outgoings into major categories, such as transportation, entertainment, clothing, gifts, and food. Once they know how much money they spend and where they spend it, they can develop a simple budget by listing their categories, deciding on a weekly limit for each, and tracking their spending.

Note: Don't forget to include saving and giving to a charity as part of the spending plan/budget!

		Amount Spent			
EXPENSE CATEGORY	WEEKLY BUDGET	WEEK 1	WEEK 2	WEEK 3	WEEK 4
Transport					
Etc.					

Remember, budgeting isn't about limiting how much you spend. It is about prioritising what you spend it on.

Before we move on, here are some recaps on debt that you need to be aware of:

- To stop debt collectors from knocking on your door, you need to pay the minimum amount required by credit providers. But to stop the debt from snowballing, you should make higher repayments, ideally paying the entire balance of your credit card off each month.
- Don't be tempted to allow your children to buy things they can't afford using 'Buy Now, Pay Later' schemes, as this is still debt and will change the cycle from 'Earn –> Save –> Give –> Spend' to 'Earn –> Spend (bills/debt repayments) -> Give -> Save (if there is any money left)'.

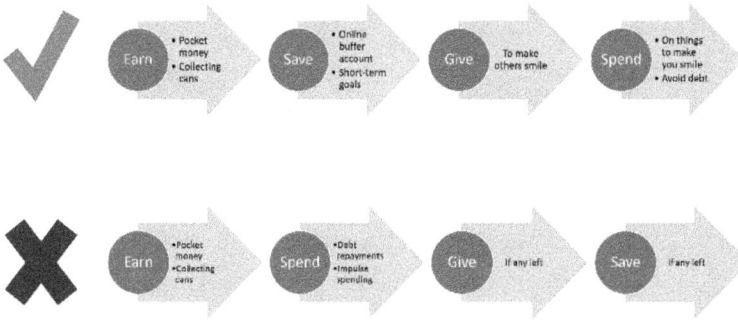

- Before starting to invest, it is important to first reduce any outstanding debt you may currently have. Debt is any amount of money you have borrowed from another person or entity, such as a car loan from dealer, credit card from a bank, or a personal loan from your parents. There are many ways to reduce debt, but the first step is always to work out how much you owe and the interest rates and minimum repayment amounts for each loan. For example:

DESCRIPTION	AMOUNT ($)	LENDER	INTEREST RATE (%)	TERM (YEARS)	MIN. REPAYMENT ($/MONTH)
Student Loan	$50,000	Big Bank	5.00%	30	$200
Credit Card	$8,000	Big Bank	19.50%	30	$200
Car Loan	$12,500	Dealer	8.50%	2	$200
Personal Loan	$5,000	Parents	0%	5	$85
TOTAL	$75,500				$685

- The next step is generally to decide on a debt reduction strategy. A licensed financial planner or an accountant will be able to determine the best strategy to suit your needs and personality, but two of the most common are:
  - The avalanche method (which pays off the high-interest debt first). Pay the minimum amount on all accounts and then put all your focus on the one with the highest rate. In the example in the above table, it would be the credit card. Once this has been cleared, put all excess funds into the next highest, (which in this example is the car loan). This method helps you pay the least amount of interest overall.
  - The snowball method focuses on paying off the smallest debt first. This allows you to gain momentum as each balance is paid off. This method is more about behavioural modification and prepares you for progressively bigger debts.
- For more information, download my top tips on reducing debt at www.kidsfinance.com.au/resources and get advice from your licensed accountant/financial planner.

Section Activities

☐ Ask your older children to record how much money they spent on a certain day and on what. Look at these expenses and determine the most common categories at the end of the week (or a few weeks). Add together the total amount spent in each category, and compare the total amount they spent to the total amount of pocket money (or their salary) they earned. Subtract their outgoings from their total earnings. Is this number positive or negative? Discuss what changes could be made to either earn more income or decrease expenses to keep the balance positive.

☐ Draw up a spending plan so your child can write their spending plan for the next month.

☐ Keep track of expenses for a month and discuss them at the end of each month.

☐ Encourage your kids to continue using a spending plan. However, remember that no two spending plans are the same, and that spending plans naturally change over time.

☐ List all sources of debt and the interest rate being charged on each (e.g., credit cards, car loans, 'Buy Now, Pay Later' schemes, and personal loans). Implement a debt reduction strategy, if required.

Key Takeaways

- Having a budget is not about being restrictive or not spending money on fun things; it's about knowing and planning what you'll pay to make sure your expenses don't end up being greater than your income (which leads to debt). Spending plans will change over time.
- Credits cards aren't necessarily bad, but they should be used with caution, and should only be given to your children when they're old enough to understand the benefits and risks associated with them.
- 'Buy Now, Pay Later' or other interest-free repayment companies make it convenient to impulse buy and, unfortunately, to start the debt cycle.

The Buffer fund can be used to avoid bad debt when required to make unexpected purchases (e.g. broken dishwasher or car repairs) but must be topped back up to desired limit before making more lifestyle purchases. Before starting to invest, it is important to first reduce any outstanding bad debt you may currently have.

10

An Introduction to Quality Assets

An investment in knowledge pays the best interest.
—BENJAMIN FRANKLIN

One of the most commonly asked questions about investing is, 'What is the best way to save and invest for my children?'—and this is one of the main reasons why I decided to write this book and share my experiences!

The next step for your children (after doing everything we've discussed in the previous chapters) is to start purchasing income-producing assets. Accordingly, the next few chapters will cover how to start investing, including opening broker accounts and using investment apps. It will also cover some investing mistakes that can be easily avoided, including information overload, finding a balance between 'my lifestyle of today' and 'investing for my future', and the fear of either missing out or making a mistake.

Unfortunately, there's no silver bullet or straightforward answer that applies to everyone when it comes to investing. I will, however, explain the strategy I used so you can see an example of our teachings in action, as well as some of the mistakes I made and learned from.

Remember, before you start investing for yourself, you should also have a buffer account and savings system set up!

Mistake #1: Not Having a Target

I knew I *should* save for the future, but I also wanted to live my best life *now*. This (i.e., not having a clear 'why') made it even harder to save (or, rather, to enjoy saving and minimise the temptation to just spend). Much like when we teach our children to have a goal that they're saving towards, we should always have a clear 'why' when we're saving and investing. After all, it's easier to say 'yes' to something that will be important to us in the future if we know exactly what that 'thing' looks like.

As mentioned earlier, I'm an engineer, and so I like to have some sort of a plan or roadmap so I can tick off milestones as I reach them—and by using the roadmap outlined in this book, although it did initially feel as though I had a long way to go, I could also see myself getting closer to my goal of living debt-free and having the option to take time off from the workforce when my children were young.

Mistake #2: Waiting for the 'Right Time'

Thinking about investing and *actually* investing are two very different things, and before I started investing, I spent a lot of time thinking I needed to save more, understand the market more, and wait for the price to decrease before I could start investing—when in fact, I actually just needed to start. That's it. Once I realised there was no 'perfect' time to start, I invested a small amount regularly and started to see results, which kept my momentum going!

The investment strategy I used was first investing in cash (always have a buffer account!) and then splitting my savings into two separate accounts: one for lifestyle items (e.g., a car; a holiday), and one for good-quality appreciating assets.

I started investing in shares. Shares don't require a large amount of money, and this was simple to automate. In this way, I slowly built up a portfolio that I then sold part of to use as my first house deposit. I then used the equity (the value the house had increased to) of my first house as a deposit for my second house and continued to invest in real estate.

Mistake #3: Not Reviewing and Adapting the Plan Regularly

My real estate exit strategy was to sell to pay for debt—that is, I aimed to accumulate enough properties while I was working and could afford the holding costs (mortgage, rates, etc.) so I could then sell them at a higher price later to reduce or eliminate the mortgages on the remaining properties. I thought that meant buying and holding for as long as possible, so I didn't think I had to review my strategy anymore, and I lost focus: by not regularly checking what the market was doing, I wasn't able to maximise on my portfolio potential. Therefore, I ended up selling one of my properties as the market was crashing instead of when it was at its highest value. The price plummeted by over one hundred and fifty thousand dollars in twelve months.

Ouch. Lesson learned.

Bottom line: money success is a momentum game. It's hard to get started, but once you get going and start seeing results, it effectively snowballs. Unfortunately, however, by the same token, if you *lose* focus, the momentum will slow accordingly, and it'll be harder to get going again. Basically, it takes commitment to take regular action.

Giving pocket money and reviewing savings goals with your children should be viewed in the same way, so schedule time in your calendar to keep things moving forward so the momentum doesn't slow for them or you.

Mistake #4: Thinking You're Alone

When you're trying to do everything by yourself, it's easy to slip back into old habits and not act—but if you have someone working *with* you who you can bounce ideas off of and who can keep you accountable, it becomes *much* easier to stay on-track. This could be a good friend or a professional advisor. Regardless of who you choose, this person should understand your situation, goals, and risk tolerance so they can optimally support you and give you confidence in the fact that you're on the right track. Professional advice can also help you to develop a unique strategy and understand all the risks associated with what you're doing (and how to minimise them). You'll be this support for your children!

Explaining Investing to Older Children

Investing doesn't require very much money for you to get started. The key is to get your children interested in and excited about investing. For this to happen, it's helpful to make it relevant to their interests: for example, for older kids into gaming, you could relate investing to playing a game, where the different commodities (cash, bonds, shares, and properties) are different players, each with varying superpowers used at different times with different effects. Each of these players also has a different risk profile (the uncertainty of the result). Some can also quickly increase in size and power (growth assets) to overpower the enemy, and some can lose all their powers if certain events happen. Others (defence assets, such as cash) steadily and confidently defend the castle against villains. The strategy of the game is asset allocation and diversification (choosing the type of commodity and how many of each type).

To 'win the game', you need to have soldiers who are always there to defend and protect portfolios. (Here, 'soldiers' represent our buffer accounts.) Emergency buffer accounts mean your children always have cash available to them, in turn allowing them to live comfortably if they lose their job due to a pandemic, become ill and can't work for a period, the stock market crashes, and so on and so forth.

Some soldiers grow steadily over a long period, and these will be sent into the field and left alone to grow and increase in power for at least ten years. Some of these will ride out the storms, some will die, and some will multiply, but overall, the army will increase in value (i.e., shares or part ownership of companies).

To demonstrate this, below is a graph from Morningstar Advisor Research Centre showing the performance of the major asset class indices over twenty years.

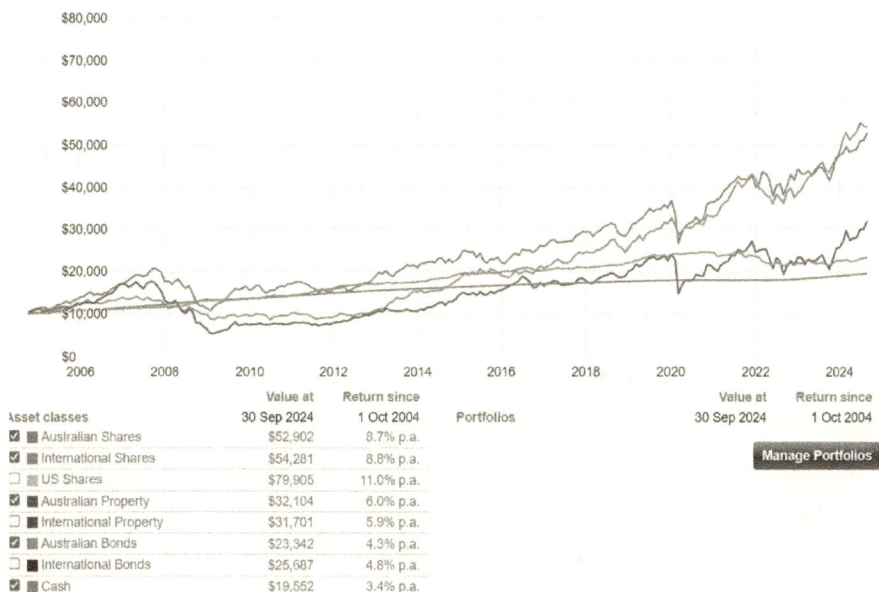

Asset classes	Value at 30 Sep 2024	Return since 1 Oct 2004	Portfolios	Value at 30 Sep 2024	Return since 1 Oct 2004
Australian Shares	$52,902	8.7% p.a.			
International Shares	$54,281	8.8% p.a.			
US Shares	$79,905	11.0% p.a.		Manage Portfolios	
Australian Property	$32,104	6.0% p.a.			
International Property	$31,701	5.9% p.a.			
Australian Bonds	$23,342	4.3% p.a.			
International Bonds	$25,687	4.8% p.a.			
Cash	$19,552	3.4% p.a.			

Source: www.vanguard.com.au

To go back to our game motif: a small number of soldiers can increase in value very quickly, but also fall in value. These soldiers might even all die straight away. An example of this might be small developing companies or cryptocurrency.

To reinforce the importance of asset allocation (i.e., how much money you're comfortable with going into defence assets, such as cash and bonds, and how much money you're comfortable with going into growth assets, such as shares), you can introduce the concept of building a model portfolio. Portfolios show how much money is currently in each asset classification. Have each family member choose a model and look at its past performance or projected future track so they can begin to understand this in practice.

There are also online investment simulators that can show the different possible results here and act as a prop for the conversation you have with your children about how they would feel if that was their real money that was lost or gained. This conversation will reinforce the concept of the risk and reward associated with investing.

Notably, there's no correct answer to the question of how much you should invest and where. Rather, this is a personal decision: only you know your risk tolerance! You can, however, get assistance from a licensed professional—but even still, the driving factor behind these decisions should be facilitating you still sleeping at night without worry.

Getting Children Started with Investing

Before we dive into how our children can start investing, let's first recap where the rest of our children's money goes—and thus where this investment money will actually come from.

As I've said, a rule of thumb we use in our family is that twenty to fifty percent of the child's money should go towards saving—and, as you also know, we pay one dollar per year of age in pocket money. However, that was under the proviso that fifty percent of this went into their 'saving' container, to be used for short-term goals. Children with a part-time job should also aim to save between twenty to fifty percent of their wages.

Our children also have an online buffer bank account, which is strictly for the future.

Overall, I recommend using a saving system that has several levels and components, such as the one shown below.

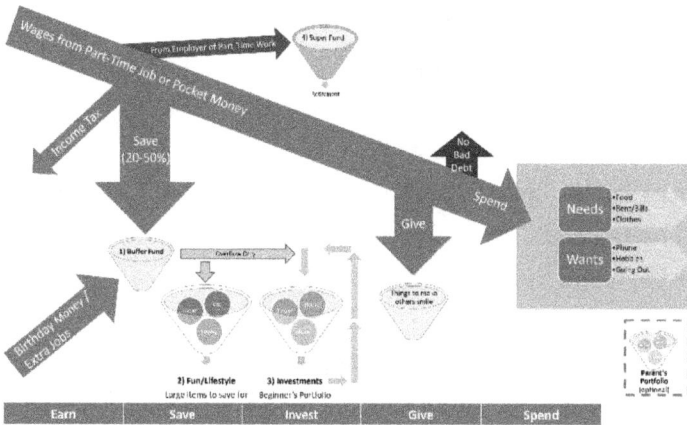

Remember, the principles of this system are the same for a five-year-old as they are for a fifty-year-old. As a reminder, these are as follows.

The Emergency Buffer Fund

The purpose of an emergency buffer fund is to ensure you always have money available if you need it.

In the case of young children, the buffer fund should be kept in the child's first bank account. This account should have no fees, and should ideally pay high interest. I notably recommend putting additional income into this account, such as gifts from relatives.

Explain to your child that this is for when they're older, and show your children the balance growing over time.

Once the children start working, set up a direct debit to be automatically collected from their salary once it hits their bank account. Having this fund already set up will form a great buffer for your children as they start their adult life, and watching this account grow over time will help them to feel prepared and like they'll never need to consider borrowing money.

The aim is to grow this fund over time, and it can and should be used as an alternative to borrowing money, such as for covering the first instalment of rent after moving out. If this money *is* used, it needs to be replenished before other big purchases are made, such as a car.

Once this fund hits the desired limit, all savings should go towards long-term investments, such as shares or house deposits. A rough guideline we use for the buffer fund is:

- Five hundred dollars for young children.
- One thousand to two thousand dollars for recent school graduates.
- Three months' worth of living expenses for those in their twenties.
- Six to twelve months' worth of living expenses for those in their thirties. (They may be married with kids at this age, so will not want to end up sleeping on a friend's couch if something unexpected happens!)

Saving For a Short-Term Goal (Fun/Lifestyle)

For young children, this should take the form of a clear plastic container that the child puts a proportion of their pocket money into. They can then watch this container physically fill up as they get closer to their short-term goal, such as a toy horse or a trip on the sky rail. As discussed previously, it's helpful to have visual aids, such as drawings or pictures, of what they're saving up for on the container's lid so they can stay excited about putting their money away and be reminded of why they're doing it.

I notably recommend that children keep this physical 'saving' container system for as long as possible—ideally, until they start working a part-time job, from which point they can open a bank account and start earning interest while saving.

For teenagers and adults, short-term goals should be saved in a zero-fee online savings bank account. This account should be used for any big purchases they're saving for, such as a new bike or a family holiday. A good tip is to set up a direct debit to automate this task, whereby a set amount of money goes straight into this account after payday. Save twenty dollars a week, and this will add up to more than one thousand dollars over the course of a year.

Investing in their Beginner's Portfolio

My children will start putting money into their investing account (Beginner's Portfolio) as soon as their emergency buffer fund is at the desired level. By doing this, my children will understand the concept of buying shares and therefore owning or being part of a company by about the age of ten.

For older children working part-time, I recommend at least ten percent of their wage going into a separate investing account—although they of course must ensure they keep topping up their buffer account to the desired level *before* they start increasing the amount directed into the investment account.

The purpose of this investing/saving is not for clothes or lifestyle items, but to grow your wealth and get financially ahead. Investing could initially take the form of saving up for a house deposit (or investment property) or buying shares/assets to make more money or make extra loan repayments (to clear any debts). As for me, I was very fortunate that my father actively invested in the share market during my younger years, so I had exposure to this early on. He also reminded me, on several critical occasions, that when investing in real estate, it is the land value that goes up over time; the building values actually go down.

The good part about investing in the share market is the fact that even when you start with very little money, you learn fundamental lessons.

To get started, every few months, the children can track the company they invested in's growth, and can receive dividends a few times a year.

Investing is also good for learning about share market cycles. A share price might be high now, but may be lower within a few months. To illustrate, below is a graph of Australia's largest listed companies (by float-adjusted market capitalisation). As you can see, there are large peaks and troughs, as well as small daily/monthly peaks and troughs.

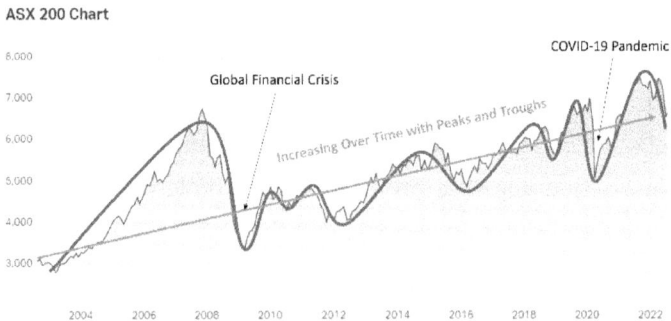

As we've covered, children have the precious commodity of time on their hands, meaning they can benefit from the compound effects of dividend reinvestment now. In mind of this, there are several ways in which you can get your children started with investing, such as buying direct shares in a company they're interested in (e.g., Disney) or buying whole or part shares in a group of companies through a managed fund or ETF. Your children may choose to continue to invest in their chosen share market for the long term (ten-plus years), or they may choose to do what I did and sell some shares to use as part of a deposit when they're ready to purchase their first house.

We will go through the different investment options for income-producing assets later in this chapter.

Superannuation (Saving for Retirement)

You may be thinking that this is not relevant to children, but actually, one of the most significant benefits of opening a superannuation account at an early age is the miracle of compound interest—and for that, you need time. And time is something your children have *lots* of.

To illustrate how beneficial investing earlier is instead of delaying contributions, let's consider two scenarios. Both assume an annual growth rate of eight percent compounded yearly.

1. The first scenario is: your child does not start adding contributions to their investment account/superannuation until they start their first full-time job at twenty-five. From this point, they contribute five thousand dollars per year until they retire at sixty-five. This results in a total of two hundred thousand dollars that has been contributed to their superannuation fund.

2. The second scenario is: your child starts contributing five thousand dollars per year from when they start their first part-time job at fifteen until they reach twenty-five, after which point no more contributions are made. This results in a total of fifty thousand dollars that has been contributed to their superannuation fund.

Interestingly, even though the person in Scenario (2) contributed only twenty-five percent of the total amount the person in Scenario (1) did, the person in Scenario (2), at age sixty-five, has a greater value, with a balance of over $1.8 million, compared to the person is Scenario (1), who has only $1.3 million.

ASSUMED ANNUAL INTEREST RATE OFF 8% COMPOUNDED YEARLY	BALANCE AT AGE 65
Scenario 1: Contribution of $5,000 per year from ages 25–65 (Total - $200,000)	$1,516,218
Scenario 2: Contribution of $5,000 per year from ages 15–25 (Total - $50,000)	$1,835,410

This shows the benefit of compound interest when you start contributing early and have time on your hands.

To illustrate further, if the parents of the person from Scenario (2) had also set up a fund at birth with a balance of two thousand dollars and made contributions of one thousand dollars per year until the child reached the age of fifteen (contributing a total of seventeen thousand dollars), the balance would double, from $1.5 million to over $3 million. Not a bad investment!

ASSUMED ANNUAL INTEREST RATE OFF 8% COMPOUNDED YEARLY	BALANCE AT AGE 65
Scenario 1: Contribution of $5,000 per year from ages 25–65 (Total - $200,000)	$1,516,218
Scenario 2: Contribution of $5,000 per year from ages 15–25 (Total - $50,000)	$1,835,410
Scenario 3: $2,000 at birth, then $1,000 p/a until age 15, then $5,000 p/a from ages 15–25 (Total - $67,000)	$3,372,369

So, how do you get children interested in saving for retirement?

The point isn't about putting all the money that you earn into superannuation (I certainly didn't); it's about knowing that *the option is there*. As with other investments, starting early and making small, regular contributions over a long time makes a huge difference. I don't recommend that your children put a large portion of their money into superannuation, as this money can't be accessed until they reach retirement age, but they should know *of* it from an early age so it's on their radar. Buying income-producing assets outside of a 401K or superannuation means they you can access the income earlier—and therefore have options earlier—but there are still some advantages to investing in a superannuation fund instead of a share portfolio. These include:

- Being able to deduct the money you're putting towards your superannuation account from your pre-tax salary. This means you will pay less tax.

- Low-income earners may be eligible for government co-contribution—meaning that when you contribute to your superannuation account, the government also contributes into your account.

- The First Home Super Saver Scheme (FHSS) means you can access any voluntary contributions (and their associated earnings) to purchase your first home. This has the advantage of tax savings as well as growth assets while saving for a house deposit. For more information on this, visit www.ato.gov.au/individuals/super/withdrawing-and-using-your-super/first-home-super-saver-scheme.

While three million dollars in superannuation does sound good, it may not be reasonable to expect a fifteen-year-old to contribute five thousand a year, or even a parent with a newborn baby to contribute one thousand dollars a year. A more achievable example (assuming eight percent compounded annually) might be parents or grandparents putting two thousand dollars in the account when the child is born and then adding only five hundred dollars per year until they started work at fifteen. The child then contributes one thousand dollars per year. This plan, with contributions totalling nineteen thousand five hundred dollars by the time the child reaches twenty-five, yields a total balance of sixty-one thousand dollars. Not a bad house deposit!

(Note: There are limitations on how much can be withdrawn on the FHSS.)

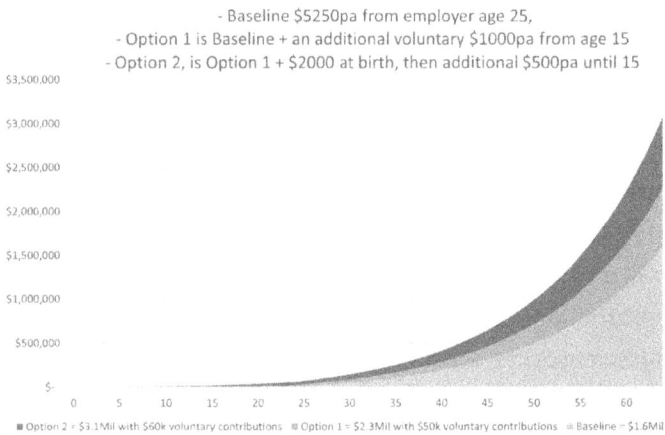

- Baseline $5250pa from employer age 25,
- Option 1 is Baseline + an additional voluntary $1000pa from age 15
- Option 2, is Option 1 + $2000 at birth, then additional $500pa until 15

So, how do you choose a superannuation account (or an investment portfolio)?

Many tools that compare superannuation products are available on the Internet, including the ATO.gov.au website, but I recommend seeking legal advice before finalising your choice. That aside, just to get you started, below are the three primary considerations you should keep in mind when choosing a superannuation account.

Fees

Minor differences in fees can have a massive impact on your balance. Even a one percent difference in prices could reduce your balance by nearly thirty percent. Let's look at this example to demonstrate:

	INTEREST RATE COMPOUNDED ANNUALLY	BALANCE AT AGE 65
Invest for 10 years at $5,000 p/a from ages 15-25	8%	$1,550,000
Invest for 10 years at $5,000 p/a from ages 15-25	7%	$1,030,000
Invest for 50 years at $5,000 p/a from ages 15-65	8%	$2,900,000
Invest for 50 years at $5,000 p/a from ages 15-65	7%	$2,000,000

That's almost *a million dollars less* in contributions of five thousand dollars per year until retirement.

Examples of superfunds with low fees are:

1. Australian Retirement Trust.
2. REST Super Index Fund.
3. HostPlus.

Investment Allocation

Try not to accept the default fund or balanced pool, as it's designed for a broad range of people and is generally more conservative in its approach to cash, fixed interest, and share allocation.

Children have the best safety net of time to invest eighty to one hundred percent in growth assets (i.e., shares; equity; property) and zero to twenty percent in defence assets (i.e., cash; fixed income). Fundamentally, though, this is a personal choice that you need to be comfortable with. Below is an example of the default lifecycle investment strategy from Australian Retirement Trust:

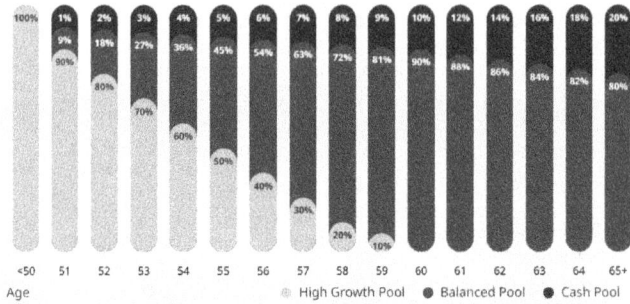

(Source: www.australianretirementtrust.com.au/
investments/options/lifecycle-investment-strategy)

Performance

The Australian Prudential Regulation Authority (APRA) does an annual performance assessment of superannuation products to improve their efficiency, transparency, and accountability. Use this assessment to ensure that your chosen superannuation product has met all the requirements. After this, you can compare the past seven, five, or three-year net returns.

Note that you also need to be aware of other things when setting up and reviewing superannuation:

1. If you purchase tailored death or total and permanent disability (TDP) insurance through your super account, ensure that your occupational rating is correct, as it significantly affects the risk profile and, subsequently, the premium amount.

2. Beneficiaries are nominated to inherit the superannuation of life insurance if you die, so make sure these are up to date. As soon as

your child has completed their estate planning or will, change this to nominate a binding beneficiary by downloading and completing the binding death nomination form from the website. The original 'preferred nomination' is used as a guide only by the trustee when deciding how to pay the death benefits. A binding death nomination will ensure that their super goes to the person(s) nominated when they die.

If you or your children's grandparents want to start making contributions to an account earlier, that's great, as one of the significant advantages to contributing to a child's super fund is its cost effectiveness. Because of this, superannuation contributions could be an excellent option for grandparents who want to give their grandchildren a head start in life. There are also many services available that make this process easy. For example:

- Golden Goose Gifting. Through studentsuper.com.au, Golden Goose Gifting currently (at the time of writing) has zero fees for balances under one thousand dollars, and balances between one thousand and five thousand dollars receive a fifty percent discount on the weekly admin fee + 0.99% of the balance. Balances over five thousand dollars have a fee of seventy-eight dollars + 0.99% of the account balance p.a.

- www.australianretirementtrust.com.au. At the time of writing, the Australian Retirement Trust has an admin fee of seventy-eight dollars per year + 0.1% and an investment fee of 0.07%-0.27% for all balances under eight hundred thousand dollars, making it a more attractive option for balances over five thousand dollars. To open an Australian Retirement Trust account for children under fifteen, a parent or legal guardian needs to authorise the membership form available for download on their website.

Both accounts have a three percent cap on admin fees for account balances sitting at less than six thousand dollars. Apart from time, one of the best reasons to open a superannuation account when children start working is the fact that you can assist them in choosing one that has low fees, the correct investment allocation, and solid performance. Once this is set up, your child can give each new employer their one preferred superannuation fund and not have multiple funds scattered here, there, and everywhere as a result of their signing up with each employer they have's default fund (which will also result in additional associated fees).

Section Activities

☐ If you haven't done so already, set up different saving accounts (or goals within a savings account) for different purposes (i.e., an emergency buffer account; a short-term savings account; an investing account).

☐ Determine the amount you are comfortable saving. This should be at least ten percent, but ideally fifty percent, of your wage.

☐ Open a superannuation account that best suits your needs. If you have more than one already open, roll these into a single superannuation fund to minimise fees.

☐ Take a minute here to think about how much debt you currently have, and how much passive income you would like to attain and by when and for how long. I have given an outline of my personal investment goals/income on www.kidsfinance.com.au; however, please seek professional advice from a licensed financial planner for your own unique situation.

Key Takeaways

- Investing should only be done after an adequate buffer account has been reached, you have no outstanding bad debt, and professional advice has been sought.
- Start investing at a level you are committed to and make regular automated contributions.
- The earlier you set up a single superannuation account which has low fees, and the appropriate investment allocation for your stage of life, the greater the chance of your investment fund growing.
- Having a plan will keep you focused on achieving your goals. Review your plan regularly and adapt as required.

11

Buy Quality Assets

Buy quality, undervalued assets.
—ROBERT KIYOSAKI (AUTHOR OF *RICH DAD, POOR DAD*)

So far, we have discussed why we need to save well, give generously, and spend wisely, and the structure for doing that. And now, the final piece in becoming financially independent is investing in quality appreciating assets.

Now, when I refer to 'assets', I mean something that will ultimately put money into your account(s), such as rent, interest, and dividends. These will initially supplement your income (wages or pocket money) and eventually replace any income you receive from doing work you don't love (though there is still no reason to quit your job if you love it and it provides the work-life balance you need).

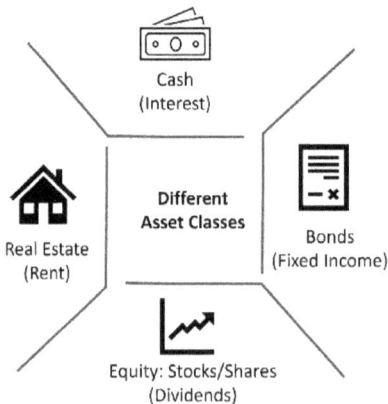

Cash
(Interest)

Real Estate
(Rent)

Different
Asset Classes

Bonds
(Fixed Income)

Equity: Stocks/Shares
(Dividends)

When considering which asset class to invest in, it is worth considering how easily and quickly the asset can be converted to cash. Non-liquid assets (known as illiquid assets), such as property/real estate, can't quickly be converted to cash, as most require the assets to be sold and ownerships to be transferred. It is for this reason that my portfolio has a mix of both liquid (cash) and illiquid assets.

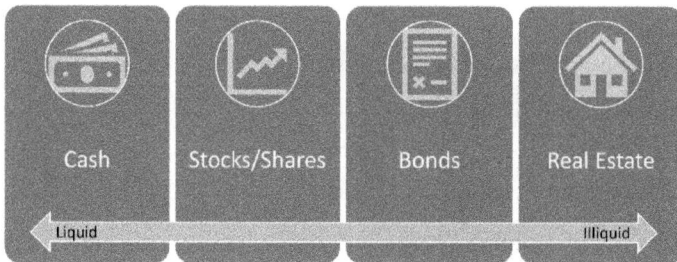

The following are a few examples of assets, and some advantages and disadvantages of each.

Cash

The most straightforward and easily attained asset is cash. The interest it pays will most likely be the first form of passive income your children receive. For your children to understand the concept of passive income, you need to show them the transactions on their bank accounts every few months. It can be exciting to see the amount the bank 'pays' increase over time as their balance increases! I vividly remember when I first realised that I was being paid 'while I slept' by simply leaving my savings alone.

The advantages of having cash are:

1. The interest can be used straight away *or* left in the account to compound.

2. Cash is liquid, meaning it's easily accessible. If you need your money, you can typically get it from the bank within a day.

3. Cash is relatively low risk. Provided it is being stored with a reputable bank, it won't disappear if the market has a sudden downturn.

The disadvantages of cash are:

1. It has a relatively low yield, meaning you won't get as much return for your investment as other asset types, so you'll need to have more of it. To find the best interest rate for your cash, you'll need to check for the most competitive rate.

2. You cannot determine the interest rate you'll receive from the bank, as the banks may change the rates as required. This means you need to know what you should be receiving, check that you were paid, and check whether there are more competitive savings accounts.

3. A bank is not infallible. Individual banks can fail, and you could lose your money as a result. However, you could have multiple savings accounts with different banks to limit exposure or lower your risk, having a max balance of, say, two hundred and fifty thousand dollars per bank.

Shares (Stocks)

Essentially, shares represent ownership of companies listed on stock exchanges. When purchasing shares, the most common strategies are to:

1. Buy and hold specific company shares in the hopes that their price will go up. They'll pay you dividends as that company succeeds.

2. Buy and hold an index fund in the hopes that the market will go up over time.

3. Buy and sell shares regularly, making a profit as the price changes (buying when the price is low and selling when the price is high).

The advantages of shares are:

1. You don't need much money (capital) to get started. Prices for individual shares can range from a few cents to a few thousand dollars, so you can always buy what you can afford at the time and invest more later. Plus, buying shares or index funds is a great way to start investing with excess funds from your online 'buffer' account.

2. Entry and exit costs are low. You'll be charged a fee (brokerage) every time you buy or sell (trade); however, as technology has changed, these have decreased a lot.

3. Shares don't require ongoing cashflow; you have the option to buy and hold and not put any further investment into them. In addition, some companies offer dividend reinvestment plans, meaning you'll receive more shares (instead of cash) over time. Hence, your holdings will increase in the same way compound interest on your bank account does.

4. The return on investment is usually higher than cash in a savings account.

5. You can buy a small piece of lots of shares in a single transaction through index-managed funds, listed investment companies (LIC), or exchange-traded funds (ETFs). For example:
   a. The ASX 200 (the Top 200 ASX-listed companies in terms of float-adjusted market capitalisation).
   b. The Dow Jones (a stock market index of thirty prominent companies listed on stock exchanges in the United States).
   c. The S&P 500 (a stock market index of five hundred large companies listed on stock exchanges in the United States).

We will go through the main differences between LIC, ETFs, and managed funds later in the chapter.

The disadvantages of shares include:

1. There is no guarantee that the company's share price you choose

will go up. There are advanced risk mitigation strategies to minimise your loss, but ultimately, you cannot control the external market.

2. Watching the price go up and down can produce stress. Only invest an amount you're comfortable with.

3. ETFs and managed funds are all run by humans, which means these people can still make mistakes, pick underperforming shares, and charge excessive fees, which can reduce your growth. Therefore, you need to research these as much as you would for individual companies.

Bonds

The third type of income-producing asset is bonds. Essentially, bonds are like loans, where you lend your money to governments, banks, or companies, and they pay you interest on the loan. Adults can purchase bonds for various amounts, durations and terms, and interest rates. The maturity date is when you will receive your money and the interest rate (or 'coupon rate', as it's called in bond terminology) back.

The advantages of bonds are:

1. They can be low risk.

2. They can give you more interest than that which you'd get from a bank.

3. The cashflow is more predictable, as the yield or interest paid will average out at the agreed rate.

4. They are relatively liquid. You can exchange or sell a bond, and you should get most or all the capital back. You will, however, forfeit the future cashflow from coupon interest.

5. There may be some tax advantages, as bonds are known as 'tax-paid' investments, meaning the tax on the earnings in the bond is

paid by the underlying fund itself. Therefore, investors don't have to declare any income from the bond in their tax return.

The disadvantages are:

1. There is no guarantee you'll get all your money back if the company or government whose bond you hold cannot pay you back.

2. The market interest rate may be higher than the interest rate you agreed upon.

Property

The fourth income-producing asset is property. This one requires a substantial amount of capital for you to start investing, and usually involves debt.

Investing in property essentially means owning buildings (either residential or commercial) and/or land in the hopes that the price or value of the property will increase over time. During your time owning the property, you'll receive rent and may make some improvements, such as renovations or block subdivisions, to increase its value.

The advantages of property are:

1. You can physically see and touch the property (thus making it feel more 'real').

2. A mortgage (a loan from a bank or institution) allows you to purchase the property with only a deposit from your savings.

3. Gaining income. Suppose the property is 'positively geared'; in that case, the rent you receive from the property will be higher than the total maintenance costs and repayments required from the bank, resulting in you receiving more income than expenses from the property.

4. If property prices go up, you can sell the property, repay the bank loan, and keep the additional funds—or you can keep the property

and use the additional equity (how much the property has increased in value) to buy more properties without saving for future deposits. There are, however, other risks associated with this strategy.

The disadvantages of property are:

1. Entry and exit fees are expensive. In addition, you need to save a considerable amount for a deposit and pay stamp duty upon purchase. You may also need to pay substantial agent fees when selling the property, along with bank fees.
2. There are ongoing expenses, such as maintenance requests, interest on the loan, council rates, insurance, and body corporate fees if the property is part of a complex.
3. You'll need to find and manage tenants for your property. You can always outsource property management to someone else, but this still costs money, and these expenses remain even when the property is vacant.
4. Property is not as liquid as cash and shares, so if you need the money back that you invested in the property, you might need to sell the property, which could take months. Plus, if the housing market is in a downturn, you might need to sell it for less than you purchased it for.

It is also worth considering the volatility and unpredictability of each of the asset classes to ensure the combination of assets is right for your situation.

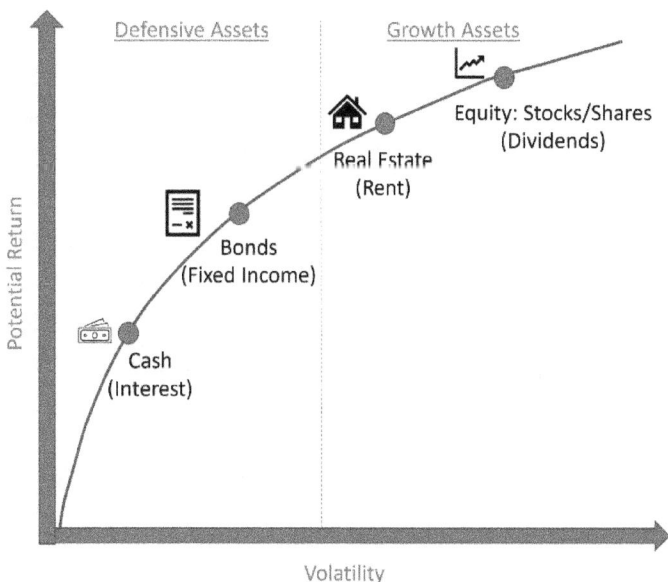

Company Shares, Managed Funds, Listed Investment Companies, and Exchange-Traded Funds

So, what's the difference between company shares, managed funds, listed investment companies (LIC), and exchange-traded funds (ETFs)?

Company Shares

Company shares represent ownership of companies listed on stock exchanges. You must purchase whole shares, and these shares can range from a few cents to several hundred thousand dollars per share. For example, Berkshire Hathaway (BRK.A) was worth USD $487,255 per share on January 18, 2022.

Buying individual shares gives you the most control over your capital, since you choose the precise company you want to have part ownership of. However, there is a brokerage fee associated with buying and selling shares. Plus, if you're just starting out, it can be costly to immediately start a diversified portfolio of ten or more shares. However, it can be a good introduction to spark interest in the share market for children. Alternatively, index-managed funds, ETF, and LIC offer investors an easy way to purchase a unit-based portfolio of securities in a single investment.

Managed Funds

Managed funds are an alternative to purchasing individual shares. A managed fund is essentially a fund that is actively managed by a fund manager who decides where to invest your money. It is an unlisted structure, which means they don't generally trade on the share market, so you will need to wait until the end of the day to buy or sell units.

An advantage of managed funds is that it effectively allows investors (you!) to 'pool' their money and have diversified portfolios. They also allow investors to make regular contributions, in turn making them suitable for dollar-cost averaging (i.e., investing a set amount of money in regular intervals).

There are generally very low or no brokerage fees for direct debit. For example, I have an automated fee-free direct debit from my bank account to our managed funds each month. The direct debit doesn't require any manual transactions or thinking on my behalf.

The benefit of investing each month (or every week) is spreading the risk of trying to time when to get into the market. I find this reduces my stress levels, since the prices fluctuate so much.

Micro-investing (more on this later) is considered a type of managed fund as it is managed by a professional and allows investments of small amounts of money regularly, often through an app that enables fractional shares or small investment units.

You can access your funds directly from the fund manager, financial advisors, or platforms, but it usually takes a few days for you to receive the funds.

Many index funds started out as managed funds. However, these days, most index funds are ETFs, as actively managed funds do not attempt to track an index; they try to outperform it!

Exchange-Traded Funds (ETFs)

ETFs are purchased and sold like shares, which means they can be bought and sold at any time when the stock market is trading and you can view the live prices immediately. Notably, you must have an account with a share market broker in order to buy and sell (more on this below).

Compared to managed funds, ETFs are more transparent about the underlying holdings. Brokerage fees are payable each time they're purchased or sold, and so may suit investors who are making more significant or irregular investments.

You can set up a direct debit to transfer funds to your cash management account each month, but if only investing small amounts, it might be more cost effective to wait for several months (until this account has a decent amount of money) before buying units so you can minimise brokerage fees (although there are some online brokers who offer very low or no fees).

ETFs also have the advantage over managed funds in that you have more control over tax payable as you only pay capital gains tax when you sell the ETF.

Most Australian ETFs are index funds that track the performance of the share market index. Examples include:

- Australian indexes, such as the SPDR S&P and ASX 200 ETF

(ASX:STW).

- The Vanguard Australian Shares Index ETF (ASX:VAS), which instead tracks the ASX 300 Index.
- U.S. markets can be covered with the iShare S&P 500 ETF (ASX:IVV).
- Vanguard MSCI International Shares Index ETF (ASX:VGAD) tracks an index that follows multiple share markets.

Listed Investment Companies (LIC)

LICs are similar in nature to a managed fund. However, LICs are always listed on a stock exchange, are publicly traded, operate under a corporate structure, and are 'closed-ended' (like an individual companies), which means there are a finite number of shares that an LIC has at one time.

An example of a prominent LIC is the Australian Foundation Investment Co Ltd (ASX:AFI), which typically invests in ASX blue chip companies.

To provide a bit more of a comprehensive summary of everything we've just covered (which is a lot!), the below table summarises some of the advantages and disadvantages of the four asset classes.

	INDIVIDUAL SHARES	MANAGED FUNDS	INDEX ETFS	LICS
On-Market Liquidity	Yes	No	Yes	Yes
Potential for Market Outperformance	Yes	Yes	No	Yes
Individual Choice Over Investments	Yes	No	No	No
Enables Investor to Pool Funds	No	Yes	Yes	Yes
Easily Provides Diversification	No	Yes	Yes	Yes

Basically, company shares, managed funds, LICs, and ETFs are all cost-effective tools for building an investment portfolio, and each are suited to different situations and needs. There is nothing wrong with investing across some or all four in your portfolio. I personally have funds across individual shares, managed funds, and ETFs!

Which Type of Broker Account to Open

A broker in the stock market buys and sells things on behalf of someone else for a fee and commission. I have used both a full-service broker (someone you can meet with face-to-face or talk to over the phone) and an online brokerage account.

The benefits of a full-service broker are that you can talk to the person and you don't need a computer or any technical knowledge of brokerage platforms in order to use their service—so full-service brokers can be a good option for people who need support in staying on top of their financial planning (outside of simple investing. The main disadvantage, however, is that the brokerage for a full-service broker is a lot higher.

Online broker accounts (such as Selfwealth and CMC Classic), on the other hand, are more cost effective, but require a little more work on your behalf to set up. There are now also many investing apps available, such as Raiz, Spaceship, and CommSec Pocket, which make investing more straightforward for beginners. We'll speak more about this later.

Note: The information and links contained in this book and on the website www.kidsfinance.com.au are not an endorsement of any particular investment products or any specific provider. It is providing information provided by suppliers. It is not providing a recommendation for your individual circumstances or in relation to any product or provider.

Opening an Online Broker Account for your Children

Shares and ETFs can be directly acquired through an online trading platform, such as Selfwealth (in 2022, the brokerage was nine dollars and fifty cents per trade for trades up to five thousand dollars) and CMC Classic (in 2022, the brokerage was zero dollars for trades up to one thousand dollars and eleven dollars per trade for trades up to five thousand dollars) and banking platforms like CommSec and nabtrade (in 2022, the brokerage was nineteen dollars and ninety-five cents per trade for trades up to five thousand dollars). Remember that a brokerage (a fee) is associated with every trade (purchase or sale of a group of shares), and so to help keep expenses down, you could purchase shares in groups instead of individually.

When you open a broking account on behalf of your child, select 'trust then minor' as the type of account. This means you operate the account as a trustee on behalf of the minor until they turn eighteen, after which you can transfer the shares into an account in their name. This will mean filling out a change of ownership, which might incur a small fee, though capital gains tax should notably not apply, as the beneficial owner hasn't changed.

You can also buy shares and ETFs in your name and transfer them to someone else's name through an off-market transfer. A fee is usually incurred with this method, however, and may impact capital gains.

This also leads us to the question of whether or not you should quote a tax file number (TFN) when buying shares. To answer this, this is your choice, but beware: your decision does affect how the tax on dividends is treated. If you mention a TFN, you pay taxes on the dividends when you lodge the tax return, and if the shares are purchased in the parent's name or by the parent as a trustee of the child and the parent's TFN is quoted, the dividends must be declared as part of the parent's annual tax return. If you *don't* mention a TFN, on the other hand, pay as you go (PAYG) tax will be withheld. In 2022, this rate was forty-seven percent of the unfranked amount withheld.

At the time of writing, if a child owns shares, their TFN was quoted when they were purchased, and they earn dividends (which are considered unearned income), worth more than four hundred and sixteen dollars per year, the parents must lodge a tax return on their behalf. These dividends will be taxed at a higher rate.

If the child earns dividends lower than this threshold, they do not have to lodge a tax return unless they earned a taxable income of greater than eighteen thousand two hundred dollars. However, you can lodge a tax return on their behalf if too much PAYG was withheld and you would like a refund on the franking credit.

For Children, in Australia, in 2022:

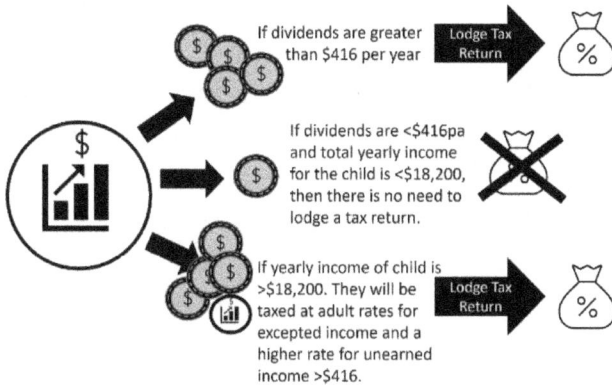

If dividends are greater than $416 per year — Lodge Tax Return

If dividends are <$416pa and total yearly income for the child is <$18,200, then there is no need to lodge a tax return.

If yearly income of child is >$18,200. They will be taxed at adult rates for excepted income and a higher rate for unearned income >$416. — Lodge Tax Return

It may also be worth investigating a dividend reinvestment plan for children. A dividend reinvestment plan (as mentioned previously) means that instead of receiving cash as dividends, the dividend is used to purchase more shares, usually at a discounted rate and without brokerage. This will increase the share portfolio automatically, in turn having the same effect as compound interest.

Most fund managers and brokers will give you an annual statement, which you will need to keep if the tax office requires you to record the date and price of the transaction.

Now, I know this is a lot of information, so let's look at some examples of this information in action:

- If parent Belinda buys shares in the name of her daughter, Georgia, from her (Belinda's) bank account, quotes her own TFN when purchasing the shares, deposits dividends into her own bank account, and uses the money for personal use, then Belinda must declare the dividends on her tax return—and when she sells, she will need to declare any capital gain or loss on her tax return.

- If Paul buys shares for his daughter, Emma, with the money she was given for her birthday, holds the shares for the benefit of Emma with a broker until she turns eighteen, quoted Emma's TFN when he bought the shares, and all dividends are reinvested through a dividend reinvestment plan, the dividends will be declared on Emma's tax returns when she starts earning greater than eighteen thousand two hundred dollars (or when dividends are greater than $416). When Emma turns eighteen, Peter will transfer the shares to her, from which point Emma will remain the beneficial owner of the shares, so there will be no capital gain or loss to either Peter or Emma until the shares are sold. Then, this capital gain/loss will be declared on Emma's tax return.

Investing Apps

This is a lot of information to take on, and so you may be wondering whether it is worth turning to the technology world to help you with this. Specifically, you may be wondering whether or not investing apps are worth it.

In a word: yes, they are worth considering. Many investing apps on the market make it simple for beginners to invest. Moreover, they're mobile-focused, which appeals to the younger generations, as this means there is no need for your kids to go through brokers or financial advisors; teenagers can execute trades from their phones with minimal capital.

Examples of some investing apps are Pearler, Sharesies, Raiz, Spaceship, and CommSec Pocket.

Some benefits of investment apps are:

- There is an all-in-one set-and-forget option: they are colourful apps that track goals easily and are visible and accessible for children.
- There are portfolio options for instant diversification:
  - Raiz, Sharesies and Pearler have six prebuilt portfolios ranging from a conservative option (mainly cash and bonds) to an aggressive option (primarily growth shares). Raiz also has an option to custom build a portfolio that allows you to include a small amount of bitcoin.
  - Spaceship has a choice of three different managed fund options. All three comprise one hundred percent stocks, so they have a slightly higher risk profile than Raiz.
  - CommSec Pocket does not have a prebuilt portfolio. Instead, it acts like a low-cost broker, allowing you to pick specific ETFs to add to your portfolio. There are currently seven different ETFs that are available to buy. In CommSec Pocket, you need to buy the entire stock, not just a fraction, like you do with Raiz or Spaceship.
- Low or no minimum investment. You can start investing with as little as five dollars.
- The ability to make regular contributions. Some apps allow you to set up an automated direct debit from your savings account to be invested automatically. CommSec Pocket, on the other hand, can automate the transfer from your account to the CommSec account,

but you must still manually select in order to invest via the app.

- The ability to make incidental contributions. Raiz became famous for its ability to 'round up' everyday purchases and invest the change. For example, if coffee is four dollars and sixty cents, you can elect to pay five dollars for coffee, and the forty cents will be invested into your portfolio. Others have have this functionality. You can turn this function on and off, which is handy.
- Low fees. Most apps generally make their money from charging a monthly payment instead of a brokerage fee per trade.
  - Spaceship fees are two dollars and fifty cents per month when you have a balance of over one hundred dollars. Notably, there are no additional fees for having multiple portfolios in Spaceship.
  - Raiz's current fees for their standard diversified portfolios are three dollars and fifty cents per month for balances under fifteen thousand dollars, then 0.275% of balances greater than fifteen thousand dollars. Both have unlimited deposits and withdrawals without additional fees.
  - CommSec Pocket have no ongoing fees like a lot of other apps. Instead, they charge two dollars per trade if under one thousand dollars, or 0.2% if over one thousand dollars.

Some things to keep in mind with investing apps before you begin using them:

- Apps can be costly if the balance invested is under five thousand (as they charge a set monthly fee).
- Your balance is visible on your phone. If you're easily stressed by market movement, watching your portfolio balance fluctuate daily may become overly worrying.
- Your funds are very accessible, which can be a blessing or a curse.
- You need to have a CommBank or CommSec account to open an

account with Pocket.

- It is difficult to view the past performance of each portfolio within the app. Most apps only allow you to view performance once you start investing.

Deciding How Much to Invest

As a rule of thumb, I recommend investing at least ten percent of your income for the building of future wealth. (Note: If you have any outstanding debt, in most cases, you will be better off paying this off first before you start saving to buy assets.)

There is no right or wrong answer to how much to invest and in which asset. The important thing is to have a plan. A plan allows you to have clear goals and targets that will give you an idea of what success looks like, and then give you the confidence to act. This will help you to overcome the challenges of:

- Information overload.
- Finding a balance between saving for your future and enjoying your lifestyle now.
- Fear of missing out or making a mistake.

Below is an example of some of potential steps to developing this plan. Remember these examples are for illustrative purposes only, and you should seek your own professional advice before committing to these steps.

- Understand your cashflow and determine how much of your income should be directed to building future wealth.
- Determine what success looks like—for example, having funds available to send your children to university while being able to work part-time or take extend breaks without sacrificing your

lifestyle.

- Set goals. For example, your goal might be to have fifty thousand dollars' worth of cash/shares by the time your child is twenty-one and to buy at least one investment property which is positively geared (i.e., which puts money into your bank account).
- Automate your savings. This involves having the correct banking structure that first uses funds to reduce bad debt with high interest. From then, you can direct five percent into increasing your buffer fund (then towards house deposit) and ten percent into an investment account.
- Find your support tribe. This could be friends, family, or professionals to keep you on-track and make sure you are set up for tax effectiveness for your unique circumstances.
- Be patient. Review at least annually to make sure your portfolio remains balanced and suited to your current situation.

To demonstrate this even further, let's look at the following examples of people in different stages of their life. Please don't compare your situation to the below examples; they are purely to give you, a parent, an overview of some different possible scenarios. There is no ideal situation for everyone. Some people have children in their early twenties; others wait until their forties. Everyone earns a different amount and can contribute to their future wealth at different rates at different stages of their life. The important message is to get started and take small regular steps.

Example 1

Tom is ten years old. He earns ten dollars per week from pocket money as well as additional money from collecting cans and doing odd jobs for neighbours and friends. He is saving up to buy his own phone for when he starts high school, and his emergency/buffer account has a few hundred dollars in it.

Tom currently splits his pocket money fifty percent into 'saving' and fifty percent into 'spending/giving'. All other money he earns goes towards his savings. His online buffer account is still a sub-account on his parents' banking system, and he has two other savings accounts (which started as containers) that he views regularly. One is his lifestyle (phone) account and the other is his investment account. Once his investment account reaches the desired limit (to minimise fees), his parent purchases more company shares (of his choice) on his behalf. He tracks the value of his shares on a spreadsheet.

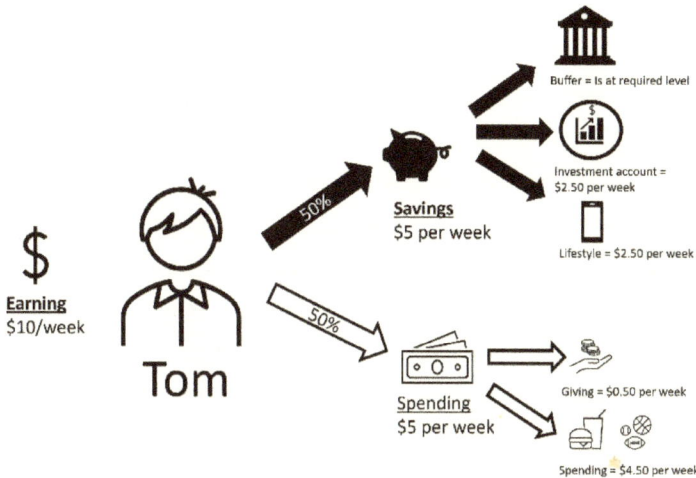

Example 2

Chloe is fifteen years old and has started her first part-time job working at the local supermarket after school and during the weekends. She lives at home, and the only bill she is required to pay is her mobile phone (eighty-nine dollars a month, or twenty-one dollars a week). She gets paid on average two hundred and fifty dollars per week after tax.

Chloe has opened a Westpac Life savings account. It has no account keeping or transaction fees, and pays 1.85% interest, provided a deposit is made each month (that is, assuming the balance is higher at the end of the month than at the beginning and the balance is kept above zero dollars at all times).

Chloe has opened a Westpac Choice everyday account to use as her transaction account. It also has no account keeping or transactional fees for customers under the age of thirty.

Chloe has decided to save sixty percent of her income, and her employer splits her pay for her accordingly, with sixty percent of the approximate total of one hundred and fifty dollars going into her Westpac Life savings account and forty percent going into a transactional account. The Westpac Life account allows her to set up to six goals, automatically distribute her savings across her goals, and track the progress of each goal.

At this stage, she has two short-term saving targets:

1. To increase her buffer account to one thousand five hundred dollars with an automatic transfer of twenty-five dollars per week (ten percent of her wage) to this goal. She will continue to slowly build up the buffer account balance over time.

2. To save for her first car, as she hopes to get her license in two years' time.

Chloe has also decided to start her investment journey using a micro-investing app, with a diversified portfolio. She has selected an option with primarily growth shares because she intends to hold them for more than five years. Her investment app account currently sits under her mother's account, but when she turns eighteen, she will automatically take over ownership of her portfolio. In the meantime, she has set up a direct debit from her savings account to transfer twenty-five dollars a week (ten percent of her wage) to be invested automatically.

As there are no transaction fees (just a monthly fee), she has decided to invest weekly to maximise the benefits of dollar-cost average. (This minimises the risk of investing at the wrong time. Some weeks, the market will be high, and others, it will be low.)

Chloe is aware of social media targeted advertising.

As Chloe only has one bill to pay (her phone), she has decided to keep all spending in one account. However, she has set up a direct debit to go out the day after payday for her phone bill.

She has an EFTPOS and Debit MasterCard attached to this transaction account. There are no fees associated with this unless it overdraws her account.

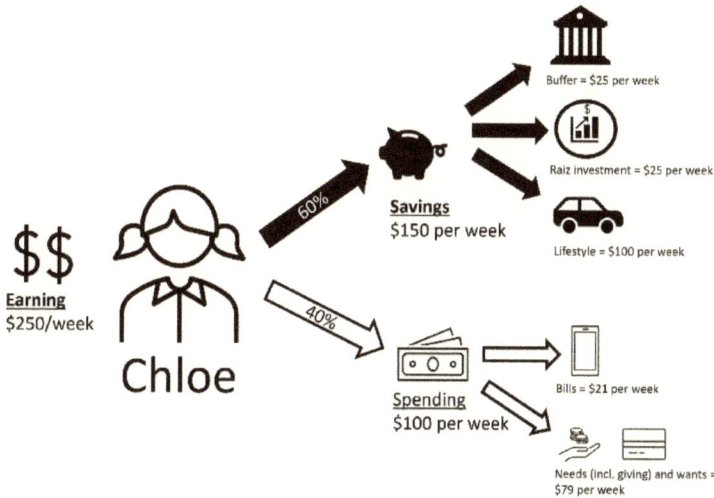

Buffer = $25 per week

Raiz investment = $25 per week

Lifestyle = $100 per week

Bills = $21 per week

Needs (incl. giving) and wants = $79 per week

Savings $150 per week

Spending $100 per week

60%

40%

$$ Earning $250/week

Chloe

Example 3

Jason is twenty-five years old and is employed full-time by the government, earning seventy thousand dollars a year. As an employee of the government, he is required to make superannuation contributions of between two to five percent of his salary (standard member contributions). He has chosen to sacrifice two percent of his salary, although if he was to increase this amount, his employer would also increase their contribution. (Note: Not all employers require you to make standard member contributions.)

He house-shares with a friend in an inner-city two-bedroom apartment, both paying two hundred dollars a week in rent. They also have electricity/utility bills of approximately two hundred dollars a week and a food bill of one hundred and fifty dollars a week.

The following table shows his income and expenses.

JASON (AGE 25)	ANNUAL	WEEKLY
Salary	$70,000	$1,346
Salary Sacrifice to Super (2%)	$1,400	$27
Taxable Income	$68,600	$1,319
Income Tax and Medicare	$14,134	$272
Take-Home Pay	$54,466	$1,047
Savings (38%)		
12.5% to Buffer Account		$135
12.5% to Investment		$135
12.5% to Savings Goal		$135
Spending		
Needs - Bills		$140
Needs - Rent		$200
Needs - Food		$150
Wants - Lifestyle Items		$152

Jason sacrifices twenty-seven dollars a week to his superannuation account. He has decided to save a total of forty percent of his salary (two percent to super and 12.5% to each of his of his saving goals). Although this is a challenging target, it is not impossible, and he knows he can always change it if he physically can't live within his means (or doesn't want to eat rice and tuna for dinner every night...). Thirty-eight percent of his salary goes into his Westpac Life savings account, and the remainder goes into his Westpac Choice transaction account.

As he is aged between eighteen and twenty-nine, he is eligible to earn 3.25% on his savings so long as his savings increase each month and he uses his debit card at least five times per month.

Jason has a direct debit set up to transfer the money needed for rent and bills to a separate account the day after his weekly pay is deposited. These bills are paid monthly so he can always make sure he has enough in this bills account to cover the set amount each month. He uses his debit card to purchase food and any lifestyle items he wants. These come directly out of his transaction account.

Jason has chosen to invest in a selection of managed funds. He has a long-term view and would prefer not to know the balance on a regular basis. He has chosen to invest directly with the fund manager and has a direct debit set up from his life savings account to transfer to the fund manager. He has chosen three different asset types (all with the same fund manager) with a different amount going into each fund:

1. Property securities.
2. Large Australian and global shares.
3. Small developing companies (higher risk).

All dividends are reinvested, and Jason enjoys his current lifestyle of living in the city centre and sharing with friends. He would prefer to invest all spare savings into the share market, as property prices are extremely high in the current market. He may decide to sell some shares later to pay for a house deposit when he is older, although this may be for an investment property somewhere else, as he enjoys being able to rent nice apartments and go wherever his job takes him.

Example 4

Helen and Roy are married and have recently bought their first house. Roy works full-time, while Helen works part-time and cares for their four-year-old. Neither has any income-producing assets but they joined their savings to buy their first house.

As their family home is not an income-producing asset, Helen and Roy wish to reduce the amount of interest paid on their house as fast as possible, but would also like to always have some cash available in case of emergencies. Therefore, they have decided not to pay off their mortgage, instead opting to pay interest only. For this reason, they have set up their home loan with their bank to have two offset accounts. (An offset account is a bank account that is linked to the home loan that you can deposit or withdraw from, in which every dollar in the offset account reduces (or offsets) the interest that is paid on the home loan.)

Helen's salary is deposited into one of the offset accounts. This is their new buffer account. They used their previous savings as the deposit for their home loan, so are now in the process of building up another buffer account.

Roy's salary is deposited into the other offset account. This is their main transaction account, and it has a credit card linked and direct debit set up for all their bills.

They are quite disciplined and can live within the means provided by Roy's salary.

By rebuilding their buffer account after it was drained to purchase a house, they will always have cash available and are less likely to go into debt. They pay for most of their living expenses with their credit card, as the bills lag by two weeks, which means they have money in their offset account for longer. (They ensure that there is always enough money in their offset account to pay the credit card amount off in full each month.)

By utilising an offset account instead of putting additional funds into paying off the mortgage, they have the cash available in case they need it. For example, if they needed fifty thousand dollars for an emergency medical operation, they could access the money in the offset account straight away and only pay the lower home loan interest rate. Alternatively, if they had paid off their mortgage, they would have to apply to either withdraw money from the loan (if it had that option) or take out a personal loan at a much higher rate, which would take several working days.

Although Helen and Roy are focused on minimising their non-deductible debt, they also realise the importance of building wealth for their future self and their child. For this reason, they are also investing in an index fund and transfer five percent of Roy's salary into this investment account. They intend to reinvest all dividends, until their child is ready to leave home, the idea being they want to have funds available to help their child start the next chapter of their life. This will not be a lump sum payout, but an incentive.

Once the buffer account is back at the desired limit, they will use more advance tax-minimisation strategies such as "Debt Recycling" to pay off debt faster and build wealth through purchasing more income generating assets such as shares or an investment properties.

Teaching their child the foundational steps of personal finance explained in Part I and then following the three rules of creating wealth explained in Part II of this book will be the best investment Roy and Helen can make for their child.

Section Activities

☐ Decide which asset class and investment vehicle you would like to invest in. Remember when doing your research to check:
  ○ The fees charged.
  ○ The asset allocation (growth or defence).
  ○ Past performance.
☐ Set up an automated amount to go to an investing account (preferably with a different institution with no fees and a high interest rate) to invest in quality assets that will grow your wealth and get you financially ahead.
☐ Set up a reinvestment plan to continually add to your portfolio at a rate you are comfortable with. Remember this can always be changed.
☐ Review your investments regularly.

Key Takeaways

• The most direct way to reach financial independence is to invest in quality income-producing assets.
• Company shares, managed funds, and ETFs are all cost-effective tools for building an investment portfolio. Each is suited to different situations and needs. Having a balance of liquid and illiquid assets will assist in building a long-term portfolio.
• Investing apps are becoming more popular. However, there are

various considerations to keep in mind before you commit to using them.

- Investing in the share market (or property) can be risky, and one needs to have a long-term view so they can ride out the highs and lows of the market without any stress.

End Note

It's never too early to start talking about money with your children.

To conclude our learnings from this book, below are the first five lessons that will set your children up for financial success while they are young, as well as the three rules of creating wealth once they start their first part-time job.

Earn

- Talk about money openly, honestly, and regularly.
- Financial independence will give you and your children numerous options in life.
- Multiple sources of income provide extra security in case something unfortunate happens.
- Talk about where money comes from and the fact that everyone must earn their money. Explain that parents go to work and/or have investments that earn them money, and so children must work hard doing jobs to earn theirs.
- Differentiate between household chores (which are expectations) and paid jobs.
- No work = no pay. If your child doesn't do their jobs, they don't get paid. Never just give your children money.

Save

- Always pay yourself first—that is, put money to the side to be saved before spending.
- Introduce the idea of goal setting and saving up for an item or experience.
- Give your child a set of three jars or clear pouches to put money into 'saving', 'giving', and 'spending'. This will become their first experience with budgeting. Explain they need to split their money between 'saving' for something important to them, 'giving' to help others, and 'spending' wisely on things that make them happy.
- Introduce 'invisible' money. Open your child's first bank account and let them watch the balance increase over time, including any interest being earned.
- Teach them about compound interest.
- Ensure a buffer fund is always available in case of an emergency.

Give

- Remind them about the importance of spending time or money to make others smile.
- It doesn't matter if you have more or less than others; you need to be grateful for the things you have, share them generously, and spend money consciously on the things that you enjoy.

Spend

- Make spending intentional, not impulsive.
- Demonstrate that money is finite: if they run out of money before

the end of the week, don't give them more (unless you're introducing the concept of interest when borrowing money).

- Explain the difference between a need and a want. Resisting the temptation of advertising can be difficult for children, but they need to know what a basic need is and what luxury items are. Even necessities need to be paid for.
- Show your children money. Let them see you hand over cash in exchange for items. Talk to your child about why you're choosing the item you're buying and explain why you didn't go for any alternatives.
- Explain the different types of money exchanges (cash vs debit vs credit).
- Give them the tools they need to understand debt.

Invest

- Start thinking about investing with your children while they're young. There are numerous options out there for starting their Beginner's Portfolio now—or you can set up a Parent's Portfolio, with a long-term view of helping them when they're older through something other than a lump sum payment.
- Avoid unnecessary debt. Save/invest at least ten percent of your income to either pay off any bad debt (such as personal loans or credit card payments) and then use this money to invest in building future wealth.
- The most direct pathway to financial independence is through investing in quality income-producing assets.

The three rules of creating wealth are...

Save (Pay Yourself First)

- Without savings, you won't be able to buy assets that will eventually produce the passive income needed for financial independence.
- Automate the transfer of savings from your transactional account to your savings account.
- Increase your buffer fund over time.

Avoid Unnecessary Debt

- Live within your means.
- Consistently put aside money for fixed bills you know are coming.
- Pay off your credit card in full every month.
- Don't be tempted to take out loans (even interest-free loans) for things you don't need. Instead, save and develop good financial habits.

Buy Quality Assets

- Income-producing assets will eventually replace your wage, giving you the choice as to where and when you want to work (if at all).
- Invest only at a rate that will still allow you to sleep at night.
- Regularly review the investments and strategies you have in place. Professional advice or someone that understands your goals and risk tolerances will keep you on track.

I hope this book has helped you understand that the financial world is not as scary as it may seem. The overarching principles of everything we have covered here are: consistent, small actions over a long time will lead to big things; and the money habits and values that you instil while your children are young and living with you will stay with them throughout their life.

More than anything, though, remember that financial independence is a continual learning journey. For a behaviour to become a habit, it must be repeated enough times for it to become automatic—so while learning about personal finance and good money habits are among the most important lessons your children will learn, they'll need to action these lessons themselves before they can begin to thrive financially.

So, now that you have finished reading this book, don't just put it down! Use it to take decisive action and change both your and your children's financial trajectory. Remember you are not undertaking this journey alone: use the resources mentioned within this book and at www.kidsfinance.com.au, including the accountability journal at www.kidsfinance.com.au/journal, and complete the activities suggested throughout this book. Generational wealth can be yours if you implement these teachings!

I wish you well on your journey to financial independence, and remember that through your progress, you will inspire others, no matter how small these ripple effects initially seem.

About the Author

Barbara Montague is a mother and author who is passionate about helping parents to teach their children about money and personal finance. This motivation inspired her to write *Kids, It's Not About the Money*, which does just that: teaches parents and teenagers alike all they will need to know to achieve financial independence (whatever that looks like for them) in a bite-sized, accessible way.

Find more information and resources for how you can teach your children the skills required for their future financial independence at www.kidsfinance.com.au.

Resources

All the Kids Finance resources mentioned in this book:
www.kidsfinance.com.au/resources

The Kids Finance Accountability Journal:
www.kidsfinance.com.au/journal

Compound interest calculator:
www.moneysmart.gov.au/budgeting/compound-interest-calculator

The Australian Tax Office:
www.ato.gov.au

Index

161, 162, 163, 164, 165, 169, 170, 190

A

assets, ix, 21, 61, 62, 63, 116, 119, 132, 137, 141, 153, 154, 156, 158, 161, 163, 165, 167, 172, 173, 178, 189, 195, 201, 202

B

bank accounts, 81, 135, 136
bonds, 27, 120, 156, 158, 176, 186
broker account, 153, 183
buffer funds, 61, 62, 72, 81, 119, 122, 135, 137, 157, 159, 160
'Buy Now, Pay Later' schemes, 147, 149

C

cash, 100, 173, 174
credit, 100, 110, 144, 145, 146, 148, 150

D

debit, 100, 110
debt, 144, 147, 149, 150
different income streams, 22, 60, 61, 62, 63, 118, 119, 131, 132, 153, 154, 155, 156, 157, 158, 159, 160,

F

financial independence, ix, 19, 22, 23, 34, 39, 61, 63, 84, 116, 131, 132

I

impulse buying, 45, 103, 104, 143
independence, 22
interest, 82, 85, 100, 145, 146, 147, 173, 174, 176
  compound interest, 27, 29, 62, 82, 83, 84, 85
  simple interest, 27, 30, 82, 83, 84
interest, 64
investing, 26, 27, 28, 29, 62, 72, 83, 84, 116, 117, 118, 119, 120, 122, 123, 137, 142, 153, 154, 156, 158, 160, 162, 167, 173, 174, 182, 187, 189
  Exchange-Traded Funds, 175, 176, 181, 183, 184
  Index-Managed Funds, 175, 176, 180, 181
  investment apps, 186, 187, 188
  investment portfolios, 26, 119, 120, 121, 122, 158, 161

Listed Investment Companies, 182
property, 177, 178
stocks/shares, 122, 162, 174, 175, 176, 179, 180, 183, 184, 185

N

needs vs wants, 106, 107

P

pocket money, 37, 38, 49, 50, 51, 52, 53, 54, 56, 57, 58, 59, 66, 67, 72, 111, 155, 158, 160

S

savings, 27, 59, 61, 62, 70, 84, 119, 132, 133, 136, 160, 189, 195, 202
savings accounts, 60, 81, 133, 136, 175, 187, 191, 192, 194, 195, 202
setting goals, 31, 59, 73, 74, 75, 76, 77, 78, 111, 112, 155, 161, 189
spending plans, 102, 110, 111, 112, 147, 150
superannuation, 63, 134, 135, 163, 165, 166, 167, 168, 169, 170

T

tax, 122, 134, 135, 184
the rich vs the wealthy, 142, 144
The Tooth Fairy, 42, 43

www.ingramcontent.com/pod-product-compliance
Lightning Source LLC
Chambersburg PA
CBHW020154200326
41521CB00006B/367